# The Dwelling Place

There is no set pattern to the unfolding of this story of a homeplace rich in memories of old friends and full living. The full circle of a year catches, in the telling, myriad refractions of the long past, to which the author has once again given life and body through the medium of her consummate art as a story-teller. With poetic delicacy and a luminous quality of writing she has quickened the past into reality.

Vachel Lindsay, William Alexander Percy, Ford Maddox Ford, Allen Tate, Richard Halliburton—these and many others distinguished in the world of letters have crossed the threshold of the Dwelling Place. Of those whose lives were intimately connected with the house, there were Lucy, Joe, Jubby the dog, Cornelia the murderess—dear familiars to Mrs. Winslow, who has touched them all with a sensitive and delicate humor.

Tragedy is here too, for sunshine has been plentifully mixed with shadow, and the serenity of the present has been won at a price. Over all is an indefinable sense of the mystic, of being just a step beyond the actual. In its own way, this is a notable interpretation of the best in Southern life.

*Books by*

*ANNE GOODWIN WINSLOW*

THE DWELLING PLACE (1943)

A WINTER IN GENEVA (1945)

CLOUDY TROPHIES (1946)

A QUIET NEIGHBORHOOD (1947)

THE SPRINGS (1949)

IT WAS LIKE THIS (1949)

PUBLISHED BY MARY WINSLOW CHAPMAN
MEMPHIS, TENN.

REPRINTED BY WIMMER BROS., INC.
MAY, 1973 MEMPHIS, TENN. 38101

# THE

# DWELLING PLACE

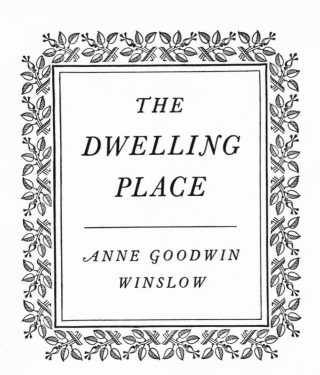

# THE
# *DWELLING*
# PLACE

ANNE GOODWIN
WINSLOW

TO

MY PEOPLE

# CONTENTS

# *THE*

# DWELLING PLACE

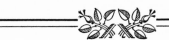

# SOLITUDE

LAST NIGHT I turned on the radio and listened awhile to *The Canary Murder Case*. I do not as a rule subject myself to either gangsters or murderers in the evenings, especially if the wind is blowing, and this time again it was a mistake. In spite of my cheerful needlework and my fire, which blazed immensely; in spite of Jubby stretched before it on his two cushions and doing all that a hundred and thirty pounds of Great Dane can do to emphasize the security of home; in spite of the *Canary Murder* itself, which was reassuringly thin and unconvincing, strange airs began to move through the familiar room, and the ivy scratching on the window-pane, as it always does when the wind is on that side, began to have a very unfamiliar sound.

By signs like these I know what a craven spirit dwells within me and what a liar I am when I tell my friends over and over, as I do tell them, that I am not afraid to live out here in this big house alone.

" And then of course there are the servants," I murmur indefinitely, with a very definite picture in my mind of Joe pursuing his night life across the fields and Lucy going sleepily to bed all those doors and rooms and corridors away.

" And of course you have the dogs," they murmur back encouragingly. " Let's see — how many of them are there now?"

And when I tell them only one, only Jubby now, they look at him as if they thought I still had dog enough.

How long would it take, I wonder, for an evil-doer, or evil-intender, to learn that most of that bulk is composed of friendliness. Mary once suggested that we tie a bell to his tail so that if burglars came his enthusiastic welcome would wag us at least a warning, but no burglar in the dictionary sense — " one who enters the house of another with felonious intent " — would be likely to choose a house as remote from the highway as this one is, and I feel pretty sure that even the casual prowler cares less for lonely places than is commonly supposed.

All the same, we have had through the years our vague alarms, our creeping terrors; emanations of the night more paralyzing than burglars because so much more mysterious, until, as almost always happened, they resolved themselves into something to be laughed at in the morning — the stealthy footsteps under the window made by a pair of visiting mules who paused there for a moment to nibble at the vines, or the phantasm of an erring possum-hunter stumbling across the lawn in the weird circle of light thrown by the lantern he carried, his bewildered dogs sniffing at his heels and his bewildered shadow leaping on ahead.

I remember one evening when I was a child there came a knock at the door much later than knocks ever came so far in the country, and I marveled in my cowardly soul at the way my father got up and went to the door and opened it quite as if it had been broad daylight. There on the threshold stood a man we had never seen before but were destined to see for some time on, for how many weeks or months I cannot now recall. Nobody asked him to stay, but since he resolutely refused to go — not only that night though my father offered him a light and a safe conduct to the road, but the next day and the next. . . .

[ 5 ]

I have no recollection of how he spent the time he so-
journed with us, but it was harmlessly I am sure, and the
shadowy figure of this uninvited guest blends uncon-
sciously with the bats and owls and other apparitions
that emerge from the deep country darkness, and sink
into it again.

We were farther from town in those days. Memphis has
grown enormously since I was a child and has unrolled
its broad highways in all directions, but in those days we
had to go and come on the " accommodation train," and
had besides three miles of dusty driving to the nearest
point where it was accommodating enough to stop. My
father, who practiced law in the city, made this journey
with great cheerfulness twice a day, but the rest of us
hardly ever went. The social life was too far away for
my mother, and the schools for us children.

Now, with everything, ourselves included, so acces-
sible, it seems odd even to me that my brother and sister
and I could have grown up here almost without companions. There were few country children near enough
for us to play with, and for this reason, I suppose, it
never occurred to us that we were country children ourselves. I don't know what we thought we were, but in
reality it must have been something rather primitive
and remote. As I look back on such an upbringing, only

the moat and the drawbridge seem to have been lacking
to make it altogether medieval.

There must have been a district school somewhere
that we might have attended, but this was apparently
not considered, and if anybody ever thought of sending
us to a boarding school, we never heard of it. My brother
was in due time sent to college as a matter of course, but
it was my father's conviction that his daughters should
be educated under his eye — though his eye was only
there in the late evenings and the early mornings. The
rest of the time we were to proceed autonomously, with
the books in the library at our disposition. I do not know
how my mother felt about this plan, nor can I remember
how we felt ourselves. My father seems to have been the
only one with ideas on the subject. There were the books,
he said, and there was he, for reference when necessary,
and if we couldn't get an education out of the combina-
tion, it was because we didn't want one.

If anyone besides my father ever saw reason to point
with pride to the results of his scholastic system, I cannot remember that either, but since it consisted entirely
in reading the things we wanted to read — out of doors,
with apples, for the most part, as I recall — it is at least
pleasant to look back on; and as I do so from this far
point in time, I realize how little a more conventional
education would have mattered after all. Certainly not

having it did nothing to shorten my sister's brief life, and I hardly see how its possession could have added much to the long happiness of mine.

Just when and by what creeping process, or what leaps and bounds, the city came nearer to us is not very clear to me now. The train was supplanted by a trolley whose terminus was only a pleasant wooded walk away; then came the highways, which threatened to come too close and didn't, and the automobiles. But before most of these things happened the books and the apples were finished; my sister had gone to Germany to study music and I had married into the army and started going everywhere. But never too far to keep coming back; with my husband or without him; with my children little and my children big, to the place that all these changes never seemed to change.

I do not see how anyone can get along without at least one thing in his life that he can think of as being both intimate and permanent. Not a mountain, though a rock might do; a tree of course is better, and a house by far the best. There he can really store his past and get at it again. Living here so much alone, as I do now, with the conditions of my life so altered that my friends all wonder how I do it, has given me a great feeling for fixtures. According to my findings they are all material, but they are very convincing to the spirit and have a power of evocation not to be denied. One stands before them like Saul before the witch at Endor: " Now bring me up whom I shall name unto thee."

When I hear people say: " Home is not the same place any more since Mother went — since Mabel married — since Rover died," I know of course what they mean and I know that they are mistaken. It is precisely because home stays the same that they are distressed about it. It is like a chain pulling them back when their thoughts want to be off in a fruitless search after Mother or Mabel or Rover — bless his heart. I always feel like telling them not to break away; to stay where they can themselves be found when the lost return.

Life with an army officer who was always moving and two army children who were always growing up, being the antithesis of permanence, made me cling the closer to the illusion of finding it here. It was a steadying experience for all of us to keep coming back and finding ourselves as we used to be. My mother and father we would find older — there came the time when we found them not at all — and there were other things to break the heart; but the sense of continuity persisted; the past was here — the cheerful past that cheerful people leave behind them. Somebody in one of the big rooms with the high ceilings was nearly always laughing. . . .

Yet the house, to look at it, would seem to have been built less for pleasure than for permanence, out of the more melancholy and monumental materials such as slate and stone, with nothing light and inflammable like clapboard and white paint, and if the ivy were not forever having its green fingers trimmed and the wistaria its long tresses shorn, the walls would long ago have been so cloaked and covered that nobody could tell what they were built of at all. I often wonder if it looks sad to people seeing it for the first time. Of course I can never see it with enough detachment to tell how it would look to me, but I am sure it has never felt sad to anyone. Perhaps if it had ever occurred to me that I would some day be living here by myself, that premonition might have cast its shadow somewhere — only I would not have believed it.

The children were both at college when their father and I finally came here to live, as the saying goes, though the illness and retirement that made this possible made it less than life to him; and now, as the other saying goes (and this time I let it stand), the children are married and gone . . . but there have been years along the way, and since these too were mostly stored up here, I am staying on.

A friend wanted to know the other day why in the world, now that I am by myself with nothing to stay at home for, I shouldn't get out and travel the way I used to do; but maybe there is nothing to travel for either, and certainly it would not be as I used to do. Traveling alone seems about as unreasonable as drinking alone. Most kinds of pleasure require company. Solitude of course does not, but that doesn't mean that it is not a pleasure. Certainly there have always been people who considered it so, and it is harder to come by than one might suppose — and steadily getting harder.

" The gift of loneliness which is the gift of freedom," wrote Chesterton regretfully, looking back on a life too full of friends. What he needed — what all such busy and friendly people need — is some way of being unsocial sociably, and I have sometimes thought, though I am not busy much of the time and friendly even less of it, that I might invent an etiquette of this sort just for the safeguarding of my unprofitable leisure; especially in the spring, when everybody wants to drive out to see the wistaria and the crab-apples and the peacocks' new tails. I have been at times so beset that I have contemplated placing some inoffensive hint or warning where guests might be reminded; not a chiming clock exactly; in the season of flowers and feathers nobody would be inside to heed it; but some good-natured and ambiguous inscription out of doors — the FAIRLY WELCOME woven into the doormat of the popular bachelor, or the famous old motto IT IS LATER THAN YOU THINK on the sundial.

There has been some very good writing in praise of the solitary life. Almost anybody might fill a five-foot bookshelf under this heading with the books he has read or " seen lying around " — Thoreau, Rousseau, Crusoe — to go chiming back into the past, with a whole catalogue of modern hermits living alone and liking it. And of course all the longest shelves are filled with the books that are the fruit of solitude, though their subject may be anything.

Perhaps if I had been more alone when I was younger (not too young), my own career as a writer might have been longer, or stronger or something. As it was, it lasted just the years the children were away at college (which were the same years), when at least I thought of myself as lonely. Certainly having them both away at once made the day seem suddenly very long and strangely silent — ideal conditions for the writing of poetry, which was the form my avocation took, and I must have worked at it rather commendably during those four years, though it ended promptly when the family education did. Mary was restored from Vassar and Randolph liberated from West Point on the same June day, and we went immediately to Europe and literature went to the wall.

But it was a career while it lasted, and fortunate as

only one so brief could be, leaving only pleasant memories behind. I loved seeing my verses in the magazines and reading the things people said about them and squandering the money I was paid for them.

" But it isn't a scarf, darling; it is a poem," I remember saying to Randolph, down from West Point, as we stepped along Fifth Avenue and saw in all the windows how beautiful he looked in the Sulka importation for which I had just exchanged a check from the *Atlantic Monthly*. I believe I enjoyed being a poet as much as anybody ever did, and this of course would be a wonderful time to " take it up " again — now with everybody gone and all my hours my own. But that was rather a good while ago and I have an idea that fashions in poetry are almost as changeable as they are in other things. Randolph wouldn't want to wear that scarf today, nor the *Atlantic* pay for it.

I can think of several reasons why poetry and I had best be parted, but none why I shouldn't take to writing prose — something long enough to be spoken of as a book, preferably a novel, or, still more importantly, as just writing. That would not only fit into my way of life but explain it. " Oh yes, she lives out there by herself," my friends could say; " she is writing a novel "; or " she writes, you know." How much better that sounds than saying she cooks, or she plays the piano, or even she reads, you know — or perhaps not saying anything and just tapping their foreheads significantly. If anyone can write a novel — if he even starts collecting the material for one — he may live henceforth as he chooses without embarrassment — in the slums, on a raft, up a tree — the odder the better, really. Saint Simeon the Stylite could have spent his twice ten years on his column without being jeered at once if he had kept a notebook and pencil well in view.

I doubt very much if I could write a novel, but I would be willing to try for the sake of all the dear people who like to worry over me. Even Randolph, who doesn't like to but who does, would worry less, I am sure, if whenever he made me a visit he found me pounding away on the typewriter in a whirlwind of loose manuscript.

When he came down from Washington to see me a little while ago — just after his sister was married — he spent most of his time pointing out to me that I have no business to be living here alone this way, and trying to persuade me to do something about it. Of course I have been here alone before, but that was in a different — a less permanent — way; only until Mary came back from somewhere, so there was something to count the days for. "This way" only means that she will not be coming back. But the days, even though I do not count them, must still be reckoned with and I think I had better stand my ground and meet them here.

She was married so suddenly, and so differently from anything I had ever imagined for her, that she seems to have been taken not only out of my days but out of my dreams, which were a wider land and occupied by her almost exclusively. This puts her for the moment very far away and creates a kind of loneliness that is new to me, and consequently difficult to cope with. But I don't believe that having people around would help very much just now — and besides, I have them. Two cousins from Nashville and one from Mississippi came for the week-end while Randolph was still here and I believe he decided before he left that what I needed was not more company but a cook, for Lucy was sick and I had only Joe to help me in the kitchen — to put wood in the stove and wash up after me while I did the more creative things.

Everybody said the shrimp gumbo and the chicken pie were better than if Lucy had made them, but it was sad to think of her stretched upon a bed of pain — all for one too acrobatic gesture after a dime that had rolled under the bureau in the downstairs guest-room. It was the Mississippi cousin's dime and she had seen it roll, but would not endanger her own vertebræ in recouping so small a sum. Naturally her remorse was great when

[ 15 ]

she found poor Lucy bent double in front of the bureau, unable to get either up or down because something had done cotch her in the back. We managed between us to get her laid out on the carpet after a fashion and covered with a steamer-rug, and then I telephoned the doctor. She wanted the rural practitioner who had once sot, and sot successfully, some bone or other in her family, but I was unfortunate enough to strike him in a good run of business and he didn't think he could possibly be with us "before dark." I was to make the girl as comfortable as possible, he advised, right where she was, since I said I couldn't move her. Better give her an aspirin.

"But I tell you she is on the floor in front of the bureau in the guest-room," I argued with asperity. "Do you want my company to have to jump over her every time they have to fix their hair or powder their face?"

This unusual aspect of the situation seemed to impress him where mere humanity had failed, for he said he would come right along.

Poor darkies — how little help there seems to be for them in time of trouble! And yet something must be kind or events would not turn out for them as they have a way of doing. Lucy was back at work again on Monday, her agony not only over but forgotten. And when one considers all that might have taken place between a bone specialist and a millionaire . . .

I am glad to be no longer cookless, for more company is impending. This is one of the seasons of the year when our friends are apt not only to come to see us but to " come by " to see us on their way to somewhere else. It is a migratory interval and we are conveniently located for breaking the trip to Florida or to California. Which is nice of course, but nicer when there is a cook.

GUESTS

"THE CORN is reaped and the earth desolate and Demeter's daughter has descended again among the shades."
This is the season of the year to remember that fateful
story, and surely it is the season of my life to try to understand it, so I have been looking into a book on Greek
religions to see what I could find. First of all, of course,
I find the usual fog that prevails as soon as we cease to
take mythology in its symbolic sense. It is strange to see
how the light goes out of it, once we begin to deal with

it as ritual or religion. Withdraw the poetic conception of any one of its familiar fables and it straightway ceases to shine. It is like moving round to the dark side of the moon and groping among the craters and cinders where once there were strange fires.

The only thing I have really learned about this myth of the Mother and the Maiden is its excessive antiquity. Demeter, it would seem, has sought her daughter under many names and by many shores — and I dare say she found on all of them kind friends to tell her she must not rebel against the course of nature and that no mother can expect to keep her children always. To which I hope she replied — in Greek, in Phœnician — in all her languages — that nobody really rebels against the course of nature; that is the march to which we all keep step, because we must, and because its beat is in our blood. It is really what seem to us the breaks in its beautiful and somber rhythm that throw us into confusion. . . .

Summer, by the calendar and in other ways, is done, but in this reluctant land the oaks still fly their colors and there is a brightness everywhere. Under the gingko tree lies a yellow prayer-rug that Joe and his thoughtless leaf-broom have so far managed to spare, and there are tawny beech leaves moving about on a very mild-man-

delightful to me; their books hardly ever; and this I regret, for it makes them think me dull or old or something, and — a little inconsistently — hurts their feelings besides. But there doesn't seem to be anything we can do about it, without too much effort and insincerity all round, so we just get on the best we can in the absence of this particular form of rapport.

I have at last got around to reading Ford Maddox Ford's *Great Trade Routes* — not because I expected to like that either, but somebody told me he had put my peacocks in it and I wanted to see if he showed them off to advantage. He found it very diverting, when he was here, to watch the way they would stroll into the hall when anybody left the door open and take their stand in front of the long mirror. Looking at themselves in any polished surface is a habit known to peacocks and long accounted to them for vanity, but what they are really thinking — if that is not too vigorous a word — is that they have met another peacock. I like what he says about them and about this place and the " tall trees thrusting their arms through heavy coats of creepers." That is wistaria, though he probably thought of it as something more " jungular." Everybody who comes south likes to think he has come farther than the vegetation really warrants. And of course it delighted me to have him remember the house as " quiet and profuse and hospitable . . . seeming to run on wheels in a deep shade." May the dear man return soon and stay longer, but never long enough to find out how far from the truth that seeming is!

The place has always played a part, and that is it: peace, leisure, time for everything; but how we poor scene-shifters have to scuffle before the curtain goes up! Armfuls of wood from the woodpile, armfuls of flowers from the garden; Lucy's egg-beater whirring in the kitchen, Joe's ice-cream freezer groaning on the back porch; and then the final burst of starched coat and cap and apron, not to mention those strategic last-minute ablutions that make in the summer-time an odd hiatus between the cocktails and the dinner gong. . . .

"Where is Lucy?" asked Allen Tate one blazing Sunday just before lunch, coming out to the kitchen to see what I was doing and finding it was the finishing decoration to a home-cured ham offered up in Randolph's honor. We even have to be " profuse and hospitable " for Randolph now that he is stationed in far places and gets home seldom.

"Lucy is upstairs taking a bath, if you must know," I answered, mopping my face. " She has to give satisfaction to my Yankee company. Yesterday after she brought the tea out on the terrace, Randolph asked me if her best friends wouldn't tell her; so I have."

" I think Lucy is always lovely," Allen said kindly.

The Tates have a beautiful old house of their own near Nashville — a high white house on the Cumberland River where it makes one of its most engaging bends.

> I have seen the poets' houses. . . .

Allen was not the poet who wrote that, but his house always makes me think of it. It would go into a sonnet very nicely, and is generally full of people who might put it there. Ford and his youthful artist wife spent a whole summer at Benfolly when he was in the South writing us up.

Judging from some of the letters I received at the time, that must have been one of those memorable intervals that everybody would be glad to forget. The last miles of any earthly journey are seldom the best, and when one has gout and asthma too, the going is particularly heavy. Poor Ford has been uncomfortable of late, here in the South as well as in other places, and his friends (he has devoted ones) have borne the brunt of a pretty wide-flung dissatisfaction.

" We are bound here like serfs to the soil," Allen wrote. " The master has suffered and we have suffered with his suffering. ' And all their echoes mourn.' . . . It is hard for our Europeans to understand that Ida (col.) or the great generic Ida can't produce Provençal cooking, and when I inquire what they would have done at Toulon if I had asked of them hot biscuit and sorghum molasses, there is no reply; and I know I have been delivering a soliloquy like the frenzied hero of a Seneca tragedy. I never realized before how indignant it makes you to have people disapprove of your food. To have the biscuits called fritters, not once but many times, seemed too insulting to be borne. . . ." Even from one whose uncle was Rossetti and who had seen Claire Clairmont plain! I wonder if he did. He told me he remembered her distinctly, though he was very young when the meeting took place, and she of course must have been very old. But even so it seems to throw an unexpected bridge across a gulf of time.

I have never known whether people expect more when they go visiting in the country than they do in town, or just get less, but whichever it is, I am sure that in the country they feel more at liberty to bring up the subject. Not only are they more confiding about how they like their food but they let you in on a variety of other tastes and prejudices and sometimes end by making you feel that you have unthinkingly lured them there under false pretenses — it is so much farther or colder or hotter than they thought it would be.

I am afraid there is one way in which I do lure them

— not unthinkingly, but from force of habit. Whenever
I hear myself inviting people to come out and spend a
"quiet" week in the country, I wonder how I have the
face to do it, being so well aware of the batteries of
sound the country is capable of turning on, for reasons
known to nature and partially learned by me, but in-
scrutable to guests.

How did the idea ever get abroad that nature is given
to tranquillity? A certain amount of self-restraint is
necessary for tranquillity, and nature has none. She is
all out and total about everything, and noisy besides,
and peace, I should say, is about the last thing on the
list of her requirements — or solitude. Nothing in nature wants to be alone for one breathing instant, and
everything that has a voice is perpetually lifting it up in
desire or bereavement, with overtones of threat or chal-
lenge, and whinnyings for help — our own unrest made
audible. I have grown so suspicious of nature's motives
as expressed in sound that only the accidental, frictional
noises — wind rustling the leaves or water slipping over
stones — gives me a feeling of repose. I made up my
mind long ago that nobody who has had much sorrow,
or even too much happiness, should ever go to the country to forget about it.

Peaceful rustic sounds indeed! Take the rooster that
comes around and crows under the windows in the

morning. That is no first fine careless rapture. Early as it is, he has things on his mind, and whether he is hurling defiance at every other rooster in the county or, as has been suggested, merely crowing the sun up — also something of an effort in its way — he is girding every feather to make good. I have explained this to my guests, but they keep on throwing their shoes at him. " ' Came the dawn ' — the din, you mean," said one of them.

And in the spring. . . . Spring of course is troublesome for everybody, but the young man's fancy, even if it doesn't always turn as lightly as the poet says, has been schooled to reticence, whereas the wanton lapwing and the burnished dove are as insistent about their emotional crises as they were at the first dawn of creation — if they were there then. I am sure that whatever was there, and singing, was doing it for something besides just joy — even the morning stars.

I came down to breakfast one lovely day in early June thinking to greet the cherished friend who had driven out from town the afternoon before to make me a visit of an unspecified number of days — long enough, we both hoped, for her to " get rested." I couldn't find her anywhere, but I found a little note from her lying beside my plate. " That peacock . . ." it was the one she had so admired in the late evening, balancing his disproportionate plumage in the oak outside her window. He had begun to scream, the note said, hours before the sun rose, before even the moon had set. She had to go home and get some sleep or she could not be responsible for her conduct as a guest or even as a human being. . . .

I knew how she felt, of course, and wrote a little note in my turn to tell her so. I knew how the peacock felt too. He was thinking of getting married, I told her, and hoped she would forgive him, but it was really a long time before she came again with a suitcase.

I am almost always contrite and apologetic about the noises, and I have lived long enough in the country and close enough to town to have acquired considerable technique in dealing with urban intolerance regarding most of the things that take place in the rustic theater of my life, so continually exposed to the comment of visitors from some city near or far; but urban ignorance concerning them still surprises me. It seems to me at times so nearly perfect as to command, if not admiration, at least a sort of tenderness. One hates to shatter it too suddenly; one is long in learning how impossible it would be to do so, how difficult to alter it at all.

I have in mind especially a certain type of educated young person with which my acquaintance was at one time rather extensive — very bright, still very young, and yet too old to learn the things that country children are confronted with so early that they never have to learn them at all. With these collegians about me I used to be reminded a hundred times a day how different is the whole mechanism of observation acquired in the fields from that acquired in the streets.

"If we are going to have supper out of doors," I suggested one summer evening to a group of young people lolling on the grass, "we had better wait until a little later — after the flies go."

"Where are they going?" asked a girl from Pittsburgh, looking up at me with lovely eyes and expecting me to tell her. I wanted to say " to the movies " or something else of a sardonic nature, but I refrained.

And I remember another time when I managed not to display my real amazement in presence of the young New Yorker who wanted to know what had happened to the moon to make it so lopsided.

"But, Harriet, you must have noticed the waning moon before," I ventured. "What did you think became of it after it was full?"

She hadn't the least idea. She had noticed crescents, she said. . . . And yet there is a moon on East Fifty-eighth Street; a lost and lonely moon, but still faithful to her phases. There must even be flies in Pittsburgh.

And here, of course, there are also the animals; the dear country creatures, so diverse, yet so familiar in the unabashed observance of their routine. I believe the ways of birds and beasts in fables could not be more astonishing to these city children, nor the *Loves of the Plants* in Darwin's epic more recondite and obscure. The fresh eggs on the table and the lovely bowls of cream have no connection in their mind with nature's maternal intentions, whether thwarted or fulfilled; and when it comes to knowing " just what exactly is a mule?" . . .

It seems somehow particularly inexcusable, in a land like ours, with its cities so newly risen from the fields, to have this cockney psychology. Young people in Europe have a very different point of view. Familiarity with the country implies for them a privileged child-hood — owning a family that owns an estate or having friends who do. Our European visitors are at home here from the start. They will not stay in the house, nor in the front yard, which is always clean, but keep getting into the back one, which is only what Joe considers so, and make their way unguided to the stable and the milking-pen.

I remember one afternoon when a friend in Memphis telephoned to ask us to help her out with some guests who were hanging heavy on her hands. " They are really very distinguished foreigners," she explained; " her father is a prime minister or something; but I don't know what to do with them, now we have finished lunch."

I suggested, as I always do, showing them Beale Street and the river, but she thought they would rather come out here. " I know you all like Italians," she added hopefully.

They proved to be delightful young people and their hostess was much gratified to find them so enthusiastic about everything in the country, but she quailed visibly when they made a break for the back gate and the horse they saw standing there and were leapt upon by all the dogs in unison. They said it made them feel as if they were at home again; and she, who knew that home was Rome, had probably been seeing them all day in the shadow of the Forum. . . .

# ANTE–BELLUM

THE SILVER TEAPOT from which I have poured more tea than it is the lot of most women to pour was presented with the rest of a rather elaborate service to my husband's grandfather by the citizens of Boston as a token of their gratitude for the benefit he had conferred on their commerce in sinking the Confederate cruiser *Alabama.* Their sentiments to this effect are engraved at some length in the center of the tray.

I cannot believe there are many persons, even in this day of rekindled Civil War sentiment, who hold any genuine animosity toward either of the opposing parties in that once famous naval engagement, but we have an occasional guest of the " professional rebel " type who through intensive fanning keeps alive sentiments ostentatiously unfavorable to the side from which my tea things came. It amuses me to see one of these visitors, after he has finished his tea and put down his cup, lean over and read the inscription on the tray and then try to look as if he had been having supper with the Borgias; but I make no comment, for I know already everything he would like to say. I feel easier with the great majority of my guests, who are not history-conscious. The engaging youth whose great-grandfather was in command of the *Alabama* when she went down has, in company with my children, consumed much food and drink seated around this trophy, entirely unimpressed even by the coincidence of his being there.

But this seems rather a pity too. I do not approve of fighting our ancient wars over again, but neither am I in favor of forgetting them, and I have sometimes thought, replenishing cups for these youthful descendants of opposing navies, that we ought to say something once in a while about that Sunday morning off Cherbourg harbor when their grandfathers were making history for them. . . .

" Officers and seamen of the *Alabama:* You have at

length another opportunity of meeting the enemy. . . . Remember that you are in the English Channel, the theatre of so much of the naval glory of our race, and that the eyes of all Europe are at this moment upon you. . . ." That was Southern eloquence, of course; but spoken by a man whose ship was steaming out to meet her doom, it might well be remembered by his grandson. And as for my own children, I was sure they had forgotten, if they ever knew, about the captain of the *Kearsarge,* who was holding morning service on his quarterdeck when the *Alabama* came on, closing his prayer-book and going below to change his Sunday cap for his old one — which was Yankee thrift and deserves to be remembered too.

Both the victor and the vanquished behaved so well on that occasion that the silver which commemorates it has always had for me a luster from both sides; but the two gallant captains have seldom joined us at tea.

I have occasionally been made to think that I missed something by not being able to get up more feeling — I mean more one-sided feeling — about the Civil War, but I believe my generation is the one that really missed that war. There had been, when I came along, just the proper time for the bleeding realities to be given decent burial and not enough for the heady growth of tradition to spring from every sod. During the years of my life when I was nearest to the catastrophe — my early child-hood — I cannot remember feeling anything at all about it except that it was a topic of too frequent occurrence in the conversation of my elders. I have thought since that those conversations must have been singularly free from emotion to have held so little interest for a child. There was, I believe, an almost invariable matter-of-factness in the reminiscences of the people, Northern or Southern, who had actually lived through those pain-ful events — referred to with a rather painful lightness as "the late unpleasantness." If the romantic aspect was already present in the minds of some of them, it was not encouraged.

I remember asking my grandmother, who lived in Nashville, to tell me about the time when she had Gen-eral Grant for her next-door neighbor. I knew that the house where he had his headquarters during the occu-pation of Nashville was separated from her home only by the yard where her lovely roses grew and the little iron fence. What did he look like, I inquired.

"I never looked at him," my grandmother answered, but so quietly that I thought she meant she was just too busy at the time, as no doubt she was, even if that was not all she meant.

For some years now I have not been able to think of General Grant in any connection without remembering about the time he appeared in a Confederate uniform on the London stage. That was in the first performance of John Drinkwater's *Abraham Lincoln,* and my friend Elisabeth Cutting, who was writing a Civil War biography herself at the time and so was especially alert to the period of the play, saw with her own eyes a General Grant in gray take over the sword of a General Lee in blue, and was naturally astounded at the sight, though she said she was apparently the only one in the audience who realized that there was anything amiss.

It was only a first-night blunder and somebody remedied it before the next performance, but of course she mentioned it a good deal in the meanwhile to her English friends, who all wanted to know what she thought of the play. Being a writer herself, and an American, her reaction was supposed to be worth something. Her reaction to the uniforms, however, turned out to be worth nothing; her friends were disposed to take exception to it and to argue the point. " I should think Drinkwater would be right about that," said a certain baronet of her acquaintance with complete finality.

I love that story; it seems to me to symbolize what I cannot help considering the artificial effort we are making these days to magnify historical and local differences which have never been so marked perhaps as novelists and historians would lead us to believe. Trying to write or even to think about the issues of the Civil War almost always ends in some sort of confusion, and while we are in no immediate danger of forgetting who wore the uniforms, I believe we often argue mistakenly about what went on inside of them.

I have done a little arguing myself in this field, especially as we see it reflected in the Southern novel, with friends of mine who are Southern and who write novels — sometimes in my house. It usually ends in a pretty animated discussion as to what constitutes a Southern novel anyhow. I am sure they are entirely sincere in believing that the literary genre they themselves have in mind when they use the term has no actual connection with the Civil War or the Negro, and that the work of Southern writers would be just as distinctive if they never mentioned hoop-skirts or corn-pone or any other of the standard properties; but all the same I am sure they are wise to go on doing it. There can be no doubt that we Southerners and the books we write about ourselves are most admired when we can be seen in all the old postures. There is such a touching determination to like us this way that many things in us and our surroundings that should have another interpretation are perpetually being construed to fit the pattern and show us as either gone or going With the Wind. And that makes me think of Mrs. Squire, who appeared in this locality just at the time Margaret Mitchell's opus was appearing everywhere.

Mrs. Squire was from New Haven, where she had prepared a paper on this prevailing work of fiction and read it before her Book Club. No wonder when she came south she was on the lookout for atmosphere, and when she got to Memphis they told her our house was the place to find it.

A short December day was already closing in when we heard the distracted honking of her automobile horn and hastened out to rescue her from the three Great Danes who were leaping like dolphins about the car, delighted with her clarion calls. She kept telling us, as we encouraged her to descend, how much later she was than she meant to be and how much longer the drive was than anybody had led her to believe, and it was quite evident that she had lost her way a good deal and must have wandered considerably — but not so far into the past as she supposed. She saw everything through an ante-bellum haze. Before we could get her in at the front door she had already looked around enough to see what was going on at the back one, which happened to be on that particular afternoon a good deal more than usual. They were putting a new roof on the kitchen, and the thing that captured her attention was a huge cauldron steaming away voluminously over a fire built on the ground, with the dusky shapes of the roof-men moving about it and stirring its contents with a stick. It was asphalt for the roof, but not to Mrs. Squire. My attempts at explanation fell on ears preoccupied with echoes from old soap-boiling, hog-scalding days on the plantation, or preparations for Saturday night ablutions at " the quarters." " Don't apologize," she murmured, " don't apologize; I find it most interesting." I was finally driven to telling her that I was not apologizing but rather boasting, since we had needed the new roof for so long, but this feeble pleasantry struck no answering spark.

We led her through the hall, where her eyes flew at once to the ceiling, which I admit is high, and then into the parlor, where, since we have no furnace, the fireplace has to be a bit on the feudal side, and got her comfortably seated by it. After which there was nothing more to do but give her tea, and that I hope was fairly up to date. It was hot, I know, and she seemed to enjoy it after her long and chilly drive, but I don't believe it broke the spell, for as she gathered up her furs to go, she asked me with disarming earnestness if she might bring her son, who would be down from Yale for the holidays, out " to see it all."

I am glad I never feel called upon to resent this type of curiosity, which, when you come to think about it, has something of the dignity of research. On the contrary, when I see it applied so whole-heartedly to such imaginary vestiges of the past, I always wish there were something more adequate I could offer — or even be. I should like to be discovered by pilgrims from New Haven still dwelling on the lee side of time, among possessions unbuffeted by the years. . . . Sir or madam, welcome to Cathay. . . .

GHOSTS

WHEN A VISITOR in the house where your family has
lived for a long time tells you with entire conviction that
she has seen a ghost, the effect is rather like that of the
last trump: the small and great rise up before you, while
you ask: which one?

My cousin Roberta, who was visiting me and who
made this announcement late one autumn afternoon,
said there were two of them — two figures, one a little
taller than the other. She had seen them as plainly as she
ever saw anything. They had passed along the lower

terrace in front of the window which was in front of her, its curtains not yet drawn.

She was quite calm about it — almost a little smug, it seemed to me as soon as I grew calm enough myself to consider it. She said they had on dark coats but didn't seem to be hurrying to get out of the rain which had begun to fall. " I thought at first it was those friends you are expecting, but I know now they were not people; they were not walking — they were gliding. But I don't mind at all," she added brightly; " do you? "

I did mind, very much. I was afraid to go out on the terrace and see, and still more afraid to stay inside and never know. I thought of some of those who, if they ever did come back, could never bear to come alone, the inseparable ones. I remembered my mother and my sister; I even thought of Mary and of me, as if we might come back like that some day. I was sure, although Roberta had not said so, that both the figures were women.

There are two terraces, one a few feet lower than the other, grass terraces bordered with ivy; and it was along this lower level, Roberta said, that she had seen them pass, going toward the front steps and the door, as if they were coming in. She thought at first they had. But when I, thanking God they hadn't, went out to look for them, the only moving objects I could see, and those but dimly, were two of my tall gray geese making their way timorously down the steps, after having, I supposed, just crossed the terrace on the upper level, which would have given them the requisite illusion of height — or so it seemed to me.

So silent were they and so completely out of place, thus far from pond and pasture, that scarcely any apparition could have seemed less likely, to a visitor at least. I, who know them more intimately, am less surprised when I meet them in surprising places, especially in this season of migration, for they too have their wanderlusts and their suppressed desires. Whatever suppressed them, I wonder. What makes them wander forth on those flapping feet when they have a wing-spread that would do for Lindbergh? Why aren't they more air-minded? I tried once to ask them these things in a sonnet. It is a good subject, but one cannot seem to address a sonnet to a goose without putting " wild " before it. " To a Wild Goose " is always good, but to a tame one, or just " To a Goose "? . . .

I brought up this subject with Roberta when I went back into the house, in an effort to divert her mind from ghosts to geese. I even read her my poem, but I found her reluctant to give up the idea that she was in touch with the supernatural. " I've seen geese before," she said, " even your geese, Anne; but I have never seen what I saw a little while ago." So after a little I gave up and went out to the kitchen to tell Lucy to bring in the tea and the Sally Lunn and the other things she had been keeping hot for some friends who were motoring through on their way to the Gulf and should have been here earlier in the afternoon.

I had never known them to be late before, I explained to Roberta, apologetically, for I knew she was hungry and had probably been seeing things on that account. We really did feel more relaxed after Lucy brought in the tray and drew the curtains and put another log on the fire, and could speculate on the lateness of our guests very complacently. Having tea by a bright hearth and wondering about friends who are out in the rain is often rather pleasant. The two on my mind just then were an aunt and a niece who lived in Omaha, but really spent their life going somewhere else in the high-powered car they drove themselves. They called this leading a wingèd existence. I had met them in Natchez several years before " doing the pilgrimage," and they had been coming by, as the saying is, to see me whenever their subsequent flights brought them within a hundred miles or so of Memphis. I felt these deviations from their trajectory to be very flattering, and so I had been willing to wait tea for them, which was a deviation on my part.

But as the evening came on and the rain kept falling and the sound of wheels on the wet gravel was still delayed, we began to wonder in earnest what could possibly have happened. After all, there were no adventures on the highways any more — only accidents — and in that case there was always the telephone. . . . Hours given to hearing imaginary horns and seeing imaginary headlights are as unprofitable as any other wasted time and not nearly as pleasant as most of it. Shortly after ten o'clock we decided to stop waiting and go to bed. It was just as I was turning off the last light that Roberta said the thing I had been hoping all the evening she wouldn't say: "But if it was a real accident, would you be notified?" she asked.

I knew of course what "real accident" meant and I knew that in all probability I would not be notified. It was very unlikely that anyone except the travelers themselves was aware of the intended detour. I could telegraph to Omaha, of course, for news, but I decided to wait until morning before doing that. There would be the paper. . . .

I had been thinking of these things, and of something else too that I didn't want to talk about, but as we separated at the top of the stairs and turned toward our respective bedrooms, Roberta put her hand on my arm.

"Anne, those two figures I saw pass the window on their way to the front door — do you suppose — ? "

I was down early the next morning to take the paper from Joe the minute he brought it from the mail-box, but there was no mention among the highway accidents of the one we feared. It was only after many messages back and forth and after what seemed too long a time that I learned where and when it happened — I believe nobody ever does learn how. This time it had been so instantaneous and complete that the question seemed irrelevant. Instead I kept asking myself how it had been possible for me to sit there by the fire all that long evening, waiting for these friends, thinking of them, talking of them, and not receive some intimation of their fate. There should have been some wave in all the ether to make me at least aware when the crash occurred and the wingèd existence ended forever in a crumpled heap by the roadside. How could it end entirely with a suddenness like that — their ardent speed — their strained intention? There must have been something that would go on. . . .

But here I had to stop. I at any rate could not go on, though I would gladly have followed Roberta in her calm acceptance of the occult. My experiences seem always to be like that; never very clear, never very helpful. The best I can hope for out of this one is to take my choice — or rather never be allowed to choose, but be buffeted back and forth forever between the absurdity of two barnyard fowls out for a stroll and a mystery so profound that the understanding fails upon its brink. But Roberta has no such conflict. She knows.

WINTER

ALL THE LEAVES have fallen; more than there were last
year, more than ever before. There is something over-
powering at times in the thought of nature's increase,
particularly when it comes tumbling down on you this
way and has to be disposed of.

Already the russet peaks and ranges are rising as Joe
and his wide rake move on down the lawn. Under the
oaks, where the fall is heaviest and every leaf an even
luggage-brown, they are so immense that they really
look like the hides of little beasts, all tanned and waiting

to be made into satchels and shoes. The piles are formidable; what is to be done with such vast heaps of anything, I ask myself every year, forgetting how they pack and shrink and take on manageable proportions after a rain or two so that they can be crammed into cotton-baskets and loaded into a wagon with high side-boards and hauled away. But not too far, for I shall want every one of them back again after it has crumbled into a little pinch of black dust, to put on some growing thing.

I often wonder if some mind, somewhere, may possibly take a view so broad and unprejudiced of all mortality and transmutation as to make even their least tolerable phases appear acceptable, as it is in the case of leaves. These are trains of thought I feel compelled at times to follow. Living as I do in the midst of plants and animals, watching the bright succession of forms that fall and rise and make their restricted cycle so many times while I am making mine once, I have need of all the consoling reflections I can muster. "You shall lie down with kings . . ." I quote from *Thanatopsis* as I pass the scarred places in the grass where something softly furred or feathered has been laid, but I can put more real harmony into the situation by remembering the loamy places in the woods and the leaf-mold scattered over the garden in the spring. No loss anywhere; only change. What a nice safe domestic feeling that gives one about this old earth that seems at most times so perilous a plank! After all, she can still boast, as the Cunard liners no longer can, that she has never lost a passenger. And if anyone doesn't find that a comforting reflection, let him try reflecting in the opposite direction and imagine getting out on some stratospheric adventure that would really lose him, so that even good old gravity couldn't get him back — not even his little pinch of dust. Imagine being drawn by the icy fingers of the moon. . . . It seems to me that any bed of earth's providing would be cozy compared to that. And the possibility of changing, like Daphne, though more slowly, into a tree — even a non-flowering one — is a tempting dream for anybody.

The trees under which I live are magnificent and most of them must be extremely old. " Did your father plant them? " one of my friends inquired, gazing with admiration and ignorance unfeigned up into the boughs of a whiteoak that must have been anything but a sapling when the Chickasaws went hunting hereabouts.

I don't think she was disappointed when I told her my father didn't. Nor was she pleased, as I thought she might be, since she is fond of me, by the implication that then I must be younger than that tall timber. She really didn't care either way; people just say those things when they come to the country.

Neither my father nor I was here to watch these trees' beginning, but I am afraid I may have to watch the end of some of them. The beech tree nearest the house, with countless names and dates cut in its silvery bark, is so old that the tree-surgeons cannot seem to encourage it to go on living, and so dear that I can hardly bear to cut it down, though it is really something of a menace to those who seek its shade. I believe it is only when disaster overtakes it that we think of a familiar tree as having a life interest of its own. Until then it has always been a background or a canopy for ours. " In youth it sheltered me," we sing; it witnessed the first kiss; it shadowed the last parting; if it could only talk, like the oak in Tennyson's poem, what tales it would have to tell! . . . It would indeed, but why should they be of us?

It can hardly be called consistent to love trees as I say I do, to agonize over their loss as I say I agonize, and then turn round and burn up whole acres of them just to keep warm — and not so very warm at that. Wood is the only thing we depend on for heating anything in this big house — either ourselves or the kitchen stove — and taken the year round, that runs into measurement at an appalling rate and sounds like a vast combustion.

I go to a good deal of trouble to explain to those who marvel at the size of the fireplaces that the trees are not cut down for us, but are already cumbering the ground that somebody is clearing — to plant more cotton, of course.

At present there are eight cords of the lovely clean stuff ranked up on the west side of the house where it will be most convenient for " toting in." It looks like a barricade, and such indeed it is, for any day now the enemy may swoop down upon us — air forces out of the north. Then the toting in will be greatly accelerated and Joe will be seen maneuvering logs as big around as he is through the doors and into the fireplaces while I scurry about the garden covering gardenia bushes and emptying pots, feeling terribly put-upon, and as much surprised as if cold weather in the middle of winter were the last thing to be expected. It is always like that, and this year my surprise and resentment will be greater than usual because of the prolonged and beautiful fall, but looking at my baronial woodpile, I can say I am for once forearmed, even if I never am forewarned.

As a rule I have the wood hauled a few loads at a time, but this was down in the bottom and Pink Ivry (I have to call him that because it is his name) asked me to let him get it all out at once before high water. Pink is black and bandy-legged and drives a truck held together — if I can say that about anything so obviously falling apart — chiefly by baling-wire. I watched him all day in a state of vicarious trepidation, and it seemed to me almost as if I were watching a miracle as load after load went wheezing and shimmying by the windows, always managing to back up at its destination before the last spasm supervened. Only once did they come to an agonizing stop right at the corner of the house and I was petitioned for a stimulating pint of gas — " so's we can jus' get around to unload."

I often feel that the difficulty that has been added to the lives of Negroes by their recently acquired dependence on the wretched derelicts they call cars and trucks should be taken into account in balancing the helps and hindrances of a mechanical age; but since they are unaware of any handicap and are always hopeful about automotive predicaments even when there is no hope, the consideration could only be one of economy, never of morale. I remember one hot Sunday afternoon spent by my cook and her companions trying to inflate the tires of a dejected Chevrolet sufficiently to get it out of the back yard and on to the main driveway. They said they knew if they could pick up enough speed for the tires to " catch the air " they would be sure to hold it. So today, though I could not help thinking how much less precarious Pink Ivry would look driving a wagon and a pair of mules, I am sure he felt highly efficient just as he was. And after all, as the December sun went down, the serried ranks of wood were there and he had gone on his palsied way home bearing a substantial check with his unbelievable name written on it, and between us we were all set for a warm and merry Christmas — the warm part mine.

As things turned out, I spent the larger part of that vulnerable interval with Roberta on her Mississippi plantation. There in the midst of peace and plenty I ate too much, slept too much, and took much too little exercise. Roberta has five thousand acres but nowhere to take a walk. The houses set in the middle of these Delta plantations, with the fields of cotton breaking up to their very doors, are strangely similar to ships on the ocean, especially at night, when each of them is a warm and pulsating unit of light and comfort and security on the bosom of a space as wide to all appearances and, originally at least, as alien as the sea. I should think the first men who started in with axe and plow to give form and feature to such limitless monotony would have expected every morning to find their work effaced by some inflowing element averse to change.

This is the time of year when, if the fields are ever dry enough for me to find a path to walk in, I always see the wagons loaded with manure moving in procession along the furrows, drawn by handsome mules and followed by Negroes in rubber boots, carrying pitchforks, to scatter on the rich earth this added richness; leaving nothing undone to make two bolls of cotton grow next year where one grew in this. Geometrical progression. Poor Mr. Wallace.

This year's crop is at least all picked and put out of sight somewhere, though the growers say they cannot sell it. But often at Christmas time the fields are still white with the summer's overflow, which nobody feels it worth his while to gather in, and then it does seem odd to watch all these preparations for more excess going patiently on. There is always the hope that the big crop and the big price may one day meet again, and that miraculous conjunction will be hailed in this region as the return to normalcy.

The Delta landscape may not encourage walking, but one could drive there interminably, following the flat unending highways on and on without ever coming to anything. No matter what the season, I remember Will Percy's poem, *Delta Autumn;* there is always that softness, that sameness, except of course in summer, when one neither drives nor walks, but does one's sweltering indoors.

Thanks to the newest highway, Roberta now lives near enough to Greenville, where Will Percy lives, for us to drive down one day and have lunch with him. We found him in the new garden with the high brick wall at the side of his house, and it looked green in spite of winter, and peaceful in spite of people taking photographs for *National Geographic Magazine*. It seemed rather wishful and pathetic for him to be having a walled garden when his heart has so wide a door. Just in the few hours we were there the doorbell rang so many times, so many times the telephone, and so many people came in without ringing anything, that I found it really distressing. I felt sure he was not strong enough to manage single-handed such a bureau of friendship and charity.

His is not one of the poets' houses. It is very large and comfortable, set back a little from the shady street, with several fine trees of its own, and I imagine anyone seeing it for the first time would be disappointed to find it so conventionally the fine house in the little town. But though it was built at a period now considered " bad " and furnished over a succession of periods none of which have been since thought " good," he has apparently never cared to change it very much, and with the exception of the garden and the library his own taste and his own experience are much less evident in his home than those of his father and mother, whose home it used to be. The acquisitions that are distinctively his have managed, in defiance of existing systems of decoration, to establish themselves without displacement of the background — the Epstein bust standing right where a bust should stand, but nothing else discarded from either strength or weakness.

Such an effect at first may not be restful to the eye, but it is very restful to the mind when one considers the peace implied in this kind of nonconformity, this absence of straining after any " period," past or future. The luncheon table was covered with his mother's long lace cloth and we ate our delicious oysters from her hand-painted plates and had a lovely party.

Will Percy, as everybody knows, is an idealist; one can tell that right away by looking at him, and, fortunately, looking at him serves to keep one reminded that idealists, even those with a fine sense of humor, are more easily hurt than the rest of us, and by more things. I have never been sure whether he would laugh or be upset if I told him something which I think very funny and which I have already told to several other people who think it funny too.

It is the sequel, in prose, to an early romance which was no doubt all poetry, and concerns a lady who when I met her, not so very long ago, could hardly have been as young nor, I suspect, as blonde as she still looked, but who was very svelte and charming in black satin and pearls and sat next to me at a women's luncheon in

Memphis. She was only visiting in that city, she told me; her home was in Greenville, Mississippi; and when I asked her, inevitably, if she knew Will Percy, she answered inevitably that she did. She had known him all her life, she said.

"He wrote some of his poems to you, didn't he?" a voice from the other side of the table inquired.

My neighbor said he had written her one — "the one he sent me from France that begins: 'When I see you I think of Mary the mother of God before she was a mother.'"

She was helping herself to salted nuts while she was saying these un-luncheon-like words and handed on the little silver dish without a flicker of any kind. And as I watched it go on down the long table, where nobody else was flickering either, I was already wondering how poets feel in cases of this kind. It may be better never to find out.

So far it has been a lovely winter; not cold, nor even as coquettish as a Southern winter prefers to be, and as I prefer to have it, if it comes to making a choice of humors. I will take all the risks of our sudden freezes for the delight of those soft days that smile between, and if I only had a more elastic system of pumps and pipes and garden equipment, my own personal adjust-

ments to the temperature would be simple indeed, regu-
lated merely by my distance from the fire.

The worst thing about the cold waves we have as they
affect my life and my behavior is the way they always
come at night. Late in the evening after a lovely day
spent mostly out of doors, the wind and the radio will
both start suddenly shrieking into my ears their warning of impending cold. Then, with the garden dark and
Joe already gone, how am I to inaugurate a mad orgy
of preparation against a twenty-degree drop in that
thermometer that hangs on the front porch and registers
my woe? About all I can do is to keep going out with
my flashlight to see how fast it is falling. I can't drain
the pump or the pipes or empty the big Italian oil jars
or even climb up into the loft to get more hay for Jubby's
house. There is nothing for it but to hope for the best
and go to bed.

But even the worst is usually of very short duration.
After a few days we are likely to find ourselves right
back again where we were before, the sun shining, the
birds singing, and the pipes either thawed out complacently or else " busted " and plugged up and waiting for
the plumber. Plumbers are as hard to get hold of out
here as doctors are; I might say, as doctors in an epi-
demic, since everybody's pipes break at once.

The fact that our water system is an individual one

and under our control alone doesn't make it any more controllable. There is the big spring at the bottom of the hill and the big tank on top of the house, and there are valves and faucets all about for watering the garden and the cows and the goldfish; but whose hand will be upon the lever in the watches of the night when certainly watching the thermometer doesn't do any good?

Hamlet's stepfather, who had learned about sorrow and spoke of it in the plural, once said: "They come not single spies, but in battalions"; and I am sure this tendency is particularly noticeable in country houses. There — not always in bad weather, but harder then to rectify — disasters seem to dam up somewhere like leaves and sticks in a stream and then break through and come rushing down on some unlucky day to make it memorable.

One comes down to breakfast as usual, on a morning that looks like any other morning, to be met by tidings such as these, in the order of their appearance:

"Somebody done lef' the gate open an' the calf done got all the milk."

"Somethin' done cotch two of them fryin'-size chickens. Mus' be a possum."

"The pump won't pump. Yes'm, I done primed it; I done done everything."

"Pearline can't come to wash; done sont word she's sick."

"No'm, the paper didn't come — less'n somebody done stole it out'n the box."

In this house the tale is generally not told until it is announced late in the afternoon — again too late to do anything about it — that the kitchen sink is stopped up. That always seems the last straw, and as a rule it is. From that low point in the scale of calamity we usually start to build up again. Occasionally, however, the movement is all crescendo and ends more nobly on the loudest note. I remember one time when a morning of such undistinguished annoyances was followed by an afternoon pitched in the mood of Bedlam, with one of the Great Danes (Jubby's younger brother Manfred) having a fit on the terrace, and another one (Jubby himself) jumping through a window-pane (six by four) and taking the greater part of it with him.

Anyone who has never seen so large a dog having a fit can hardly imagine the sound and the fury of it. I had never known its like before, and neither had Jubby. We were both of us frightened out of our wits, but I had the advantage of being inside the window, which was closed, while he was outside on the terrace with the whirling, foaming, howling Manfred. His immediate impulse being to come where I was, he came the shortest way, which led him right through the window glass.

Why we were not both of us terribly cut I have never been able to figure out. The whole room was full of glass. There were even splinters of it out in the hall, where Jubby ran for refuge and shrank and trembled in a corner of the stairs until I could get around to consoling him with the remains of yesterday's roast, after poor Manfred had recovered from his fit and been put to bed in the garage.

The mess was all swept up in time and sheets of wrapping paper pasted over the wide aperture which now framed the rising winds of March — there would be of course the usual delay about repairing any damage in the country. And then a slow rebellion that had been smoldering in me all the morning took the violent form of making me just turn my back on a life that had become too much for me and walk out of it.

I didn't walk far; there were not very many hours left and the best thing I could think of on the spur of the moment was to go to town and spend them in a manner as different as possible from the way I would spend them at home. I will go, I said, and take a look at how the other half lives — the people who really accomplish something and don't waste their time nursing sick darkies and sick drains and mad dogs. . . .

So I sought out a friend who had just published a novel and was already writing another one, under conditions carefully ordered to be as favorable as possible to the undertaking. She had given up her house and rented a small apartment in rather a slummy part of town where she would not have to know her neighbors; where, without a servant or a telephone, creation could have its unimpeded way.

It was a hideous little hide-out, but we burrowed immediately into her manuscript and only stopped once to make tea over a gas ring and shake some dry little cakes out of a paper bag, until we had finished reading all she had written and it was time for me to go home.

A healing experience, but not quite in the way I had intended, for the field of combat from which I had ignominiously fled seemed rather splendid to me when I returned to it in the windy twilight and saw the blue smoke from my high chimneys curling about the treetops and blowing westward to the early moon. Compared to writing a novel in a stuffy room that smelled of gas, there was a sort of wild glory about living in a place where I could be so vast; where I could have chimneys so high for logs so huge to burn in; windows so wide for Danes so great to jump through. . . .

I was, for the time being, quite enamored of the scale on which my agitations moved.

SPRING

WE HAVE BEEN nursing Jubby through pneumonia — a very sudden and serious attack — and now that he is definitely out of danger — out of the house even, and sniffing about the garden in the spring sunshine to check up on the rabbits that have been there while he lay abed — I find myself meditating a good deal on the nature of joy.

It is a subject about which I should know more than most, having had in my life more than the usual allotment of the various forms of happiness, and I flatter myself I am becoming even more intimately acquainted with it as these forms assume the more intimate character that goes with their diminishing proportions.

There seems to be so little difference, subjectively considered, between one joy and another. The disparity between the delights of our youth and those of our later years lies only in the number and the nature of the objects we consider at different epochs to be worthy of such vibrations, and not in the vibrations themselves. This is naturally a personal point of view, but it is, as I have indicated, the opinion of an expert. Sir Philip Sidney said something in a sonnet about being " long with love acquainted," and this has been my case with joy. How well I know the rustle of those wings! Once it was pearls from Samarkand that they denoted; now it is Jubby getting well, but inwardly the message is the same.

The night we saw him through his crisis was appropriately but inconveniently stormy. The little white-breasted birds that every year choose the vines over the windows as a wayside inn on their journey to wherever they are going at this season were quite literally upset by the whipping of the ivy branches, and kept dashing themselves against the window glass and fluttering up and down it like distracted skaters on the ice. They seemed more than ever on this anxious night to " mean something" by their behavior, but however ill-omened they might be, I did not want to see their fatal presages fulfilled on them, so I sent Lucy to call the cats into the kitchen and leave them there, cuddled as is their silly wont under a perfectly cold stove, while the windy hours went by and we sat in the parlor and kept the fire blazing. For that is where the sufferer lay, of course, in his accustomed place before the hearth, with extra rugs and cushions around and beneath him. Joe had given him his tablets for the night and poured the final bottle of milk and whisky down his throat, and so departed, leaving Lucy and me alone to share the long watches.

"If you'll s'cuse me, Miss Annie, but you rubs the misery back into him ef'n you don't take your hand up every time," criticized my assistant, who sat watching my efforts with the camphorated oil and making involuntary motions with her hands in the right direction every time I moved mine in the wrong one.

"All right, Lucy, you take it over," I answered miserably, thinking it made little difference who did the rubbing and whether right or wrong, so low poor Jubby seemed. The doctor had said he didn't have much of a chance, his years being so against him.

But, as doctors sometimes do, he underestimated something; love, perhaps, or Lucy, for before the night was over she had rubbed her patient back to life.

"Miss Annie," she called, "he's up and walkin'. Mus' I let him go outdoors?"

And outdoors he went, for a long drink of water from the fountain on the terrace. In the light from the windows he looked like some foolish and fantastic beast out of a child's picture book, with his front legs through the sleeves of a padded pajama jacket and a leopard skin from a worn and ancient coat dangling about his shoulders.

Even the wind and the rain could hardly hurt one so miraculously restored, it seemed to me, and of course neither he nor Lucy saw any reason why he should not go as usual to the fountain if he wanted a drink. The fact that he could neither stand nor stagger all the day before was already erased from their consciousness, as it deserved to be. I was the only one who remembered it, and it made me feel strangely unworthy. Even Joe, when he came in the early dawn to be greeted by a risen Jubby, seemed not particularly surprised. Was sick — is well. . . . What a pleasant conjugation, and how naturally accepted by those who are not grammarians!

One of my Christmas presents — the nicest one — was a basket full of hyacinth and tulip bulbs. All the while I was waiting on the weather, I kept it where I could look at it and think how reasonable and sure was the hope it contained. I never knew a bulb to break its promise, unless it happened to be eaten by a mole.

Moles are a destructive force in my garden. I have set a price upon their head, and Joe is winning his way to fame and fortune by an extraordinary skill in catching them. He doesn't wait to go for a hoe or spade or any other implement, but just stamps his heel, bare or shod, into the track where he sees one of them plowing and cuts off its retreat. Naturally the little beast cannot make much speed ahead where the ground is still untraveled, and it is a small matter to disinter him and pick him up by his little stump of a tail and bring him, still blindly paddling his four little feet " as one that beateth the air," to the lord of the vineyard, who am I, and claim the reward, which is twenty-five cents.

To say the price is on his head is only a manner of speaking, for it is really on the whole small varmint. I ought to have them skinned and make a coat out of their beautiful soft pelts, but I cannot bear to do it. Instead, Joe takes each one of them off in a bucket and deposits him somewhere far away; at least such are his orders. I only see them depart in their tumbril and hope that no worse fate than homesickness awaits them at the end of the trip; but some day Joe may absent-mindedly appear in the moleskin coat.

I gave him for Christmas the elegant remains of the

fur-lined leather one Randolph and I purchased in
Vienna back in the brave days of inflated kronen, when
a dollar would purchase anything, and I remembered
how we made a joke of smuggling it through the cus-
toms of those small new states of which we had so lately
heard that we did not feel in the least respectful toward
their frontiers. How much we are hearing of them now!
When will we cease to hear?

There are two white figures in that enclosure where Joe
and the moles and I all find so much to do. One is the
goddess Flora, too small for an outdoor statue (but who
wants an indoor one?), tucked away rather, at the end
of the least used walk, where she can hold her marble
garland aloft with her good arm and hide her bad one
behind a cedar bush and look as silvan as possible. Perhaps when she takes on more of the nice green patina
she is slowly assuming, I shall be able to give her a passing glance without remembering the tiresome shops
gleaming with such replicas all over Rome and Florence,
from one of which tourist traps she came no doubt,
though not to me.

For my other classic shape I take the full responsibility. It is a baptismal font from some ruined church.
There is one bad scar, discolored as if by fire, on its curv-
ing lip, but it is otherwise undamaged and the mocking-

birds and cardinals have delightful baths in it when the cats are busy watching something else.

Its graceful presence among the lilies doesn't seem a bit out of place, and one curious thing about it which no one has yet explained to my entire satisfaction is that we never have to empty it or put oil on it or have the least apprehension that it will be a breeding place for mosquitoes; and this, in a climate where even a spoonful of water left standing can make night hideous, is not an unimpressive miracle, though it is perhaps presumptuous to claim it as being worked in my favor when it is manifestly unfavorable to wiggletails. These trains of thought are bound to end in confusion. " Not a sparrow " is about as low in the biological kingdom as it is safe to follow them, and my fountain's immunity had better be explained by some allergy or other. Perhaps mosquitoes do not like the lime in marble, or the oil in magnolia leaves. There is an overhanging *Magnolia nudiflora,* and I know it would be lovely if I might be permitted to give christening parties out there for the youngest generation. I can imagine the flecks of light and shadow — even the white petals — falling on the babies and on the long white robe that has done duty so many times in the family, but never out of doors.

It was used last for last summer's baby, Randolph's son; and Pearline, who does the washing beautifully,

" did it up " for the occasion with much pride, but also with considerable confusion.

" It isn't soiled," I explained as I gave it to her, " only yellow, so don't rub it. You can see how old it is. The baby's great-grandfather was baptized in it," and I displayed its archaic dimensions, holding my thumbs through the armholes and shaking out the embroidered skirt, which hung down much longer than my own.

Pearline, who is a Baptist and not a realist, looked very much astonished. " Lawd, Miss Annie! " she said. " Wasn't his arms mighty little? "

Never having heard before of an infant " joining the church," she must have had some grotesque, not to say terrifying vision of the grandfather, an infinitely old and weazened man, going down into Jordan miraculously arrayed in the garment I was giving her to wash.

It was white and fair when she brought it back to me, with only a little too much starch, and it was nice to know that no ancient controversy need be opened between Pearline and me concerning the ceremony for which it was intended. We were equally sure that it was meant for the best and could do no harm to the initiate, whether young or old.

Along the garden walks the daffodils are gleaming. They come so much before the swallow dares, one trembles at their daring. I can never forget a fatal spring when they stood there all in bloom and every one encased in ice, like a yellow candle in a hurricane shade.

That was another cold wave that came at night, when it was too dark in the garden even to see the lighted daffodils. But if I could have seen them, I couldn't have picked them all and brought them in; there were too many, and the house was already full to overflowing with spring flowers — the long switches of forsythia and the stiff branches of *Pyrus japonica* and the magnolia buds, brought in to open in the warmer air. Besides, it had been pouring rain for days, and everything was soaked with the water that was getting ready to 'freeze them in.

The sun came out after all the damage was done and spring had disappeared from the earth, and there was something almost hateful in its indifferent splendor. We had company that day — some people from Chicago who had just arrived and wouldn't believe me when I told them all those 'flowers in the house had come out of the garden. They could see the garden through the window from where they sat by the roaring chimney, but there was not a speck of color in it, for the ice might almost as well have been fire, so brown and ashen were the tracks it left. Their incredulity was so genuine that it really cheered me up a bit and I led them about through the rooms, showing off my rescued blossoms as Noah might have exhibited the embellishments of the ark.

No other ides of March that I remember brought disaster comparable to this, but it is a tricky season, as everybody knows, and those who seek their happiness in gardens ought to cast about for something to fall back on at this time of year. But what? It is hard to be philosophical when one's vernal hopes are put suddenly into reverse. Even religion rather fails in a case where Providence is so plainly to blame. I have found a good deal of comfort in recalling the pensive blasphemy of a neighboring farmer who remarked — he was sitting on his little front porch at the time, watching the river climb out of its banks and make its way over his newly planted fields: "Taking the Lord up one side and down the other, He does about as much harm as He does good."

That is a point of view which I can sympathize with even if I do not quite agree; for, after all, spring does come on forever, as the poet says, and no matter how much it trips and stumbles, manages somehow to bring its burden of beauty in.

The poet who said that was Vachel Lindsay. He was here one lovely day in one especially lovely spring and we stayed out of doors the whole time, walking about

and sitting on benches and listening to him talk —
which he did in prose, of course, but somehow as if it
might turn into hexameters at a moment's notice, like
Homer.

A young writer of my acquaintance was telling me
not long ago about some interesting material for a paper
on Vachel Lindsay that had come his way — a romantic
bit of personal history and some unedited letters; he
thought almost any of the literary reviews might like
to have it, but I was not so sure. The old admirers have
something else to admire by this time and I doubt if
there are many new ones. The next time I had a group
of young collegians handy, I took a small plebiscite
among them, with very discouraging results. He had
once great acclaim from college audiences.

The afternoon he was here, he noticed, as we were
strolling about, a place where the terrace had just been
mended and the concrete was still wet enough to make
marks on — a temptation to anybody. He looked around
for a sharp stick and set to work to inscribe his name.
We would have liked very much to have it there, with
the day and the year cut deeply and permanently in one
corner of that artificial stone, but his expressiveness
knew no corners, and the arabesques and flourishes of
his autograph covered so many square feet of the surface
at his disposal and looked so odd when completed that

we were not sorry to have a rain come up in the night and wash it all away. Writ on water after all. . . .

There is only one brief interval in any spring when my garden seems to me to be what gardens in other places must be a great deal oftener or they would never have acquired such a reputation as haunts of peace. I refer to that fleeting space between the coming of the flowers and the onrush of the weeds. The weeds grow faster, but the flowers come first, and there is one immaculate moment — it seems no more than that — when we may stand among them with clean and folded hands who all the rest of the summer will be standing among them on our heads, groveling at the weeds.

I admit the necessity of weeding; I must even, in spite of the position involved, admit its dignity since it is this prerogative of choice, between the tares and the wheat, so to speak, that makes a garden out of a wilderness, and a gardener out of a man, but beyond that and the fact that it is good exercise, there is little I can say in praise of an occupation so hardening to the heart. I think a woman is at her worst when she is seen tearing and snatching at vegetation which, however she may call it, is often as innocently lovely as the *Herrenvolk* to which she gives the name of flowers.

I let Joe take over most of my weeding, and the fact that, in spite of all I can do to him, he is still a man and not a gardener is perhaps one reason why my garden is so seldom one of those lovesome spots of which God wots.

Nevertheless it has always been able to boast of two " cash crops " — the lilies of the valley and the gardenias. They are usually in great demand for spring weddings and have been long and favorably known to the flower shops in town; but like most earthly things, both good and bad, they all happen at once and we can never sell or use or give away enough of them to lift the clouds of fragrance that hang too heavy on the air during the weeks of their profusion.

It is the gardenias that really besiege and invest us with their perfume, for they have to be cut every morning and brought in out of the hot sun, and when I look up from my breakfast and see through the dining-room window more huge bridal bouquets coming down the garden walk clasped in the arms of Joe, I cannot be as happy as I should. I know that everything in the house that will hold water is already full of them; we have to take them out of the bathtubs, unless we want to bathe with them (as Cleopatra would have done I suppose); and the goldfish in the fountain stick their little noses up between gardenias all day long. We banned them from the icebox long ago because the cream and the butter got so permeated with them. It is too much sweetness to experience, but not to look forward to, nor to regret.

Once when we had the gardenias and the magnolias and the full moon all white together, we gave a party and added white dresses to the effect. There should always be figures moving in a garden, preferably young ones. There should always be figures, whether they move or not; even something stationary on a bench, or a statue — even Flora. That is one reason why the strictly formal garden is so effective; it is designed to throw into relief these contrasting forms.

But when I say I want people moving in my garden, I should like to make it plain that I want them to move on the walks and not over the beds — a thing they are especially given to doing in the early spring when the beds still look so empty. My mother used to say that whenever she heard of people who were supposed to have the " growing hand " with flowers, she always wanted to state her own preference for the growing foot — for those who look before they leap.

All the loveliest things on the place are a heritage from her growing hand. They are her flowering monument and keep her always here, so that it seems strange ever to take them to that place where she is not.

Today I cut the first asparagus, away ahead of the calendar because of the warm winter. It takes a good eye and, more important still, a good memory, to find these earliest shoots, coming up as they do among the tulips and the peonies and looking exactly like them. The asparagus has its own bed, of course, but refuses to lie in it, and goes sleep-walking all over the garden and crowding in among the other things, where we would never see it if we didn't remember just where to look. Even so, plenty of it manages to escape and shake out its green plumes and be very ornamental as a background for the flowers, or as a foreground for cavernous summer fireplaces later on. I suppose we all learned about putting asparagus in the fireplace from our grandmothers. I know mine always did it. It used to mean summer to me when I was a child.

When I come into the kitchen in the spring, bringing the first pearly tips of asparagus or the earliest little peas — both looking so much more like a vernal offering than like something for lunch — and turn them over to whoever happens to be cooking for me, I always wonder how I can bear to leave them in hands so unordained. So much can happen to them before I see them again and so very little should; they would be delicious just as they are. But when you say " boil " to the incumbent of the average Southern kitchen, you should always indicate the difference between spring's green jewels and the weekly wash.

The incumbent of my Southern kitchen is today less than usual in a state of mind to be entrusted with anything so fair and frail as the first asparagus, owing to an adventure of a most unusual nature that befell her in the night. When I came down to breakfast I was met with strange tidings indeed. I, who never have burglars, have had one. How much of a one I shall never know, I suppose, for he was scared away in the initial stages of his undertaking and had only penetrated as far as the storeroom, where he was fortifying himself with the contents of the refrigerator before proceeding farther (on his stomach, like Napoleon's army), when he heard Lucy stumbling down the back stairs, whereupon he fled, carrying with him, of all things, a blue china pitcher full of cream and two fresh eggs. It was certainly a mild and innocent selection compared to the roast of beef and other virile articles on the same shelf. But I believe even the best-balanced burglars are temperamental about what they choose to steal.

Lucy can hardly bear it that he got away before she saw him. "It's just about somebody we knows, Miss Anne," she keeps saying. "Look how he went right by Jubby's house and Jubby didn't even bark; and how he knowed right where the light was, and propped the door open with the little steps, just like we always does."

It was hearing the door-spring "crying" that woke her up, she says, and it was only because she caught her foot as she descended and clattered down the stairs that he took fright and ran before she could see which of our acquaintances he was. So preoccupied is she with this personal, I might say social, aspect of the adventure that she does not seem to share in the least my feeling of horror at the idea of that dusky figure, known or unknown, prowling about in the darkness and consuming dairy products in furtive gulps.

I wonder what I would have done had I come upon him thus engaged. Would George, who rakes leaves for me in the spring, or Freddy, who cuts the grass in the summer, or Pink Ivry, who hauls the wood in the fall, have still looked meek and manageable to me under those sinister circumstances?

I can only hope I would have said something forceful and authoritative — "What are you doing here at this time of night?" for instance — and not have screamed or run, which would have greatly embarrassed any future relations between us.

On the whole I am glad to be left in ignorance of the thief's identity. It is so much easier just to hold them all potentially guilty and not quibble over details of individuality. Now, with all the spring work coming on and the spring guests impending, is no time for casuistry. There is too much for them all to do. Of course there remains one clue outstanding that may yet place the guilt on one specific head — the blue pitcher. Lucy or Joe may see it again some day, doing duty in the house of a friend, or if he cracked it in making good his escape, being used as a mantel decoration. If they do I hope they will forget to tell me.

HOUSECLEANING

IT HAS BEEN too wet to work outside so I have begun that atavistic ritual called spring cleaning, which in a house as big as mine means going over ground so little traveled by anything except spiders and silver-fish that I am surprised every year to find myself there again and inclined to wonder whether these forced recognizances are really necessary. But necessary or not, there I am, scaling closets and plumbing chests, with Joe and the vacuum cleaner following at my heels like a mechanized division that will soon pass over me and keep on, leaving me bogged down somewhere in my excavations. These occasions somehow never fail to bring to light things of extraordinary interest to me, though it would never cross my mind to visit them at any other time. And every year when it is all over and everything back exactly as it was before, I have the same delightful feeling of accomplishment.

All women will tell you how " grand " they feel after a prolonged bout of housecleaning, and most of them believe this is because they know that now the house is clean, but I believe it is really because they haven't, so to speak, been there while it was going on; they have been having a complete change of scene, which is always a benefit, no matter what the scenery.

A friend of mine, a Frenchwoman, came in one afternoon much invigorated by a long walk in the cemetery, where she had gone, she said, *pour changer les idées;* and that is exactly the process involved in most domestic upheavals. We should think of them as substitutes for travel — awakening, as most of them do, all manner of foreign sounds and smells. Anyone who has to stay at home and doesn't want to should start making alterations on his house. Even such minor ones as painting and papering leave monotony immediately behind, and nothing he can get on board of will take him farther from home than putting into it one of those things known as a permanent improvement. A new floor or another bathroom can keep him a pilgrim and a stranger for weeks together.

I have a delightful neighbor with a perfect passion for this sort of architectural jouncing, and since neither her imagination nor her bank account ever seems to run low, she leads a genuinely nomadic life moving from room to room in her own house — leaving, like the nautilus, her low-vaulted past for the more stately quarters she is forever building.

There was one time, however, when I went to see her and found she had reversed the process and was going in a subterranean direction. I was greatly startled, as I let myself in at the front door, to see from the hall her head and shoulders appearing without the rest of her above the floor in one corner of the dining-room — like Rhoda the Mystery in the side-shows of my childhood. She was descending a new circular staircase leading downward through the solid earth to the " rumpus room " (also new) somewhere below.

Just looking on at things like that is quite a tonic in the dull stretches when nothing is going on under my own roof; but just now I am straightening out the books and having almost too much variety. I should like to have somebody explain to me why, when there are so many chances against any book proving interesting, the dusty ones read standing in a dim light are nearly always impossible to put down. These frequent halts were a great nuisance in my army days, when the shelves all had to be emptied in a hurry because the quartermaster's men were there putting the books in boxes to be shipped; but now the books do not have to travel any more; they just stand there waiting to be dusted and I am the one that gets shipped. This time it was to Italy, in *The Enchanted April,* one book I should read over every year whether I dust it or not, just at this season when spring nearly always suffers a backset and our own April seems to be turned around and going the other way.

I know the villa at Porto Fino that is supposed to be the setting for this story; I have two paintings that came from there, hanging now one on either side of the window through which I can look out on my sloppy garden. They were no longer in the villa when we found them, for that had been sold to a German plutocrat and much of its furnishings moved out to make room for his plutocratic belongings. A little antique shop in the village had acquired what it could of the villa's faded splendor, these two pictures among the rest.

They looked so especially forlorn standing with the other homeless objects on the dusty floor, accumulating bumps and bruises on their beautiful goldleaf frames, and we could see so perfectly how they would suit those two high spaces on our parlor wall, that we decided to undertake the business of patiently and expensively unwinding Italian red tape in order to get them on a ship at Genoa and our own red tape to get them off again at New Orleans. How patiently and expensively we could only learn as we went along.

But I used to notice that if I never bought anything in another country except under conviction of its appropriateness to some special niche in my own life, then even the most devilish experiences in getting it home would leave no blemish on it. All the curses in all the custom houses would fall away from it as soon as I saw it in the place for which it was intended, and it would bear henceforth only its early and romantic association.

A connoisseur might think these pictures needed something in the way of romantic association to make up for what they lack as art. They represent two rather corn-fed cupids toying with roses and musical instruments against a background of Renaissance architecture, and they are, as far as I can see, entirely without meaning, unless the contrast between the infantile voluptuousness of the bambini and the motto each displays on a lettered ribbon waving about his middle and constituting his only garment counts for something. These inscriptions are in Latin and presumably from the Bible.

"Watch," says the one I am able to translate, "for you know not the day nor . . ." The rest is lost behind a dimpled knee. Foolish enough, and yet for some reason, claiming so little as works of art, they leave the imagination free to wander in the far and pleasant places they recall. The granite headland at Porto Fino, for instance, where the enchanted villa stands, and the road that winds up to it, between the equal blue of sea and sky, along that Ligurian profile which must be as beautiful, and I should say as Greek, as anything in Greece.

If I were asked to name quickly the supreme loveliness of earth, I think I should say I used to see it there, through olive trees. It is those worn and weary little trees that make it so intensely lovable. Old apple orchards have much that same way of bringing beauty home; but the olive, being so rooted in antiquity, is a more sustaining symbol of ancient and pastoral things.

A modern Italian poet, Francesco Pastonchi, wrote a beautiful sonnet about olive trees which I translated once for an American magazine. No translation is ever good in the sense of the original poem, and I have forgotten just how bad this one was, but the next time I am digging for something among the magazines heaped up in the tower room, I intend to look for it.

The tower room is in the center of the upstairs, and instead of being used as a sort of dry-dock for derelict literature it should be converted into a studio or laboratory of some sort because of the even light that never fails beneath its high glass roof. It has been selected as a workshop many times by creative guests, but they invariably feel themselves too much withdrawn and soon come down to " work " more sociably on a lower level.

While it is waiting to be the cradle of a new masterpiece, the old ones that everybody is through with keep mounting higher and higher around its walls, which seem to be gradually closing in. Even the spring cleaning falters on the threshold of the tower room, where dust has attained a kind of dignity, and the periodicals that contain my literary output belong to years already deeply overlaid. I always hesitate to stir them up; after their fitful fever they sleep well. . . .


This morning I opened the door of the downstairs cupboard where we always put the things we think we have finished with before we are sure enough to relegate them to a remoter limbo, and there on a shelf between the telescope and the mah-jongg set lay the white mask of Richard Halliburton.

I knew it was there, of course; it had been there ever since the winter we had the life-mask party; but it startled me because I had been reading so much in the newspaper about Richard and his little cockleshell of a sampan adrift on the Pacific in latitudes unknown. I have steadily refused to believe he is lost. He will turn up on a coral reef somewhere, living off of something, and I only hope he doesn't have to wait too long to get the papers, for he would love to see how full they have been of him.

He was telling us the plan for his Magic Carpet adventure the evening we made the mask; and before the plaster even had time to set, he was off and gone. When he came back, after so long, and from so far, nobody remembered to give it to him, and so we have it still.

All the other victims of that evening's entertainment could hardly wait to claim their reward for the ordeal of lying stretched out on a table with straws in their noses while the grease and gauze and plaster were smeared over their faces and everybody made remarks about their features. I wondered how they could feel rewarded enough when they saw the finished product, though several of them looked quite lovely in their pale semblance of sleep. Richard's was one of the good ones and I was conscious of an almost superstitious start, coming suddenly on this cold presentment of his ardent young face.

Rainy days, and this is one of them, are not the days to go poking about in cupboards and closets and stirring up the past — even the very recent past. I should like to always do housecleaning in bright weather when there is plenty of sun to dry the tears of things, but of course I never can, for those are the days when everybody has to work in the garden. So today, having started badly, I have just gone on from bad to worse, falling finally into that nostalgic slough, a trunkful of old letters.

The faded ribbons and the dry rubber bands that tied them into packets came apart, as they always do, almost before I touched them, and shed them on the floor in heaps — leaves from the deciduous past. Why does one never have the strength of mind to scoop them up and put them back into the darkness instead of taking them to a better light near the window and coaxing them back to life?

My thoughts being already directed toward the Orient by Richard's adventure, it was inevitable that I should choose first from the scattered envelopes one postmarked Singapore, the last letter we had from another friend of ours who " journeyed toward the east," not on a magic carpet nor in a sampan; by conventional modes of travel, but a fabulous journey none the less.

There are many snapshots of Clarke Knowlton about the house. Every now and then one falls out of a book when somebody opens it — a young man in a soft shirt or a sweater, romping with the dogs, making a crack shot at croquet, eating sandwiches under the pecan tree.

There are none that show him writing stories or dreaming of the East.

We knew about his stories (which came out in the magazines) and various other distinctions which he never mentioned — his Croix de Guerre and his Prix de Rome — all easy things that had come his way. But nobody ever mentioned his Oriental streak, as we called it when we learned about it later. I believe most of his friends never knew about it at all.

It was a curious, metaphysical sort of thing. I think the nearest he ever came to explaining it, even to himself, was in a story he wrote for *Scribner's* about a little boy who exasperated his parents by telling them fantastic tales of things he thought he had seen and they knew he never had — all of them tropical and Oriental. We didn't care for the story, and it was so completely unlike his other work that I rather suspected there was something behind it. There was a pathos about his little boy that smacked of the autobiographical; and Clarke finally told us that his own psychology had been split like that when he was a child, between two entirely different sets of phenomena whose reality to him was identical. The little boy in the story died, as I remember, but Clarke merely grew up and left such things behind. He was a delightful realist when we knew him. The letters he wrote us one summer when we all went away and left him in charge of the loose ends of this big place enchanted us with their comprehension of its problems — the ones we had gone away to get a rest from, but still liked to hear about.

9 p.m. of a quiet Sunday. So far all goes well. John seems recovered after a bottle of Grove's chill tonic (which he took all at once) and there really was no reason why he should set in for a course of chills, so he didn't. The cat has not sneezed. Diane the Dane thrives on attention and is forever leaving her nose in doors. Such a soft nose too! This place is an endless joy. I have not been off of it since you left. Have adopted your suggestion of using the big table upstairs to write on. . . .

We came back to find everything in the house, animal and human, improved by our absence, but in spite of the big table, Clarke's novel had not grown. I urged him to stay on after he delivered the reins of government back into my hands, promising to ensure him uninterrupted hours, promising even to hang his meals in a basket on his doorknob when he did not feel sociable. But that was the trouble; he always did feel sociable, and though he did stay on awhile, it was not to write.

It was then I began to notice that there was something seriously the matter with the muse. His projected novel was abandoned and several short stories (better than anything he had ever done) were left in that half-finished state that always seems, when anything is good already, to promise infinite excellence. Yet he was always well and apparently not unhappy. It was as if he were merely waiting for something.

I wanted very much to help him over this interval of inertia, and since I could not furnish inspiration, I proffered the sympathetic interest I sincerely felt and led him on to talk whenever he would.

I was sitting in the hammock sewing, on one of the autumn mornings after our return, and he was sitting tailor-fashion on a wide and backless bench under the same tree. He had on a slip-over sweater with broad bands of color, russet and dull yellow, in the sort of design we see in Persian rugs. His outdoor summer had made him very brown indeed.

" You look like a would-be Buddha," I told him, " sitting that way with those hieroglyphs all over you. Did somebody give you that sweater or did you feel a call to pick it out yourself — the call of the East? "

" I picked it out. I really am Oriental, you know," he said seriously.

" *Entendu* — but how come? Which one of your ancestors is responsible for that side of you? " I wanted to know what there could possibly be in Clarke's nice average-American family to account for his extraordinary prepossession. But although for once he seemed

[ 93 ]

willing to talk about it, he could give me no light from that direction; he was entirely convinced himself that it was not a question of heredity.

We didn't see so much of him as the winter came on and his idle open days in the country had to be exchanged for days in town, which he liked much less, and the social activities he had always disliked with an intensity worthy of something a great deal worse. But one didn't have to see him much to realize that he was restless and unsettled; still waiting for something, it seemed.

He never said anything about going away. I knew there were many reasons why that would have seemed impossible to him just then; but I was sure he wanted desperately to go, and I thought that I knew where.

Then one afternoon in February, one of those first miraculous afternoons when the sun, instead of dropping like a shot behind the trees, slips in like a bright guest for tea, we saw Clarke walking rapidly up from the gate. He had telephoned that he was bringing tremendous news, so we were not surprised that he had his passport in his pocket. The way had been cleared for him in a moment of pure magic, he said — " but Cinderella knew she would have to be back at midnight and for me it will maybe be a year — all the summer and the winter — Egypt, India, China. . . ."

His letters from these places began almost at once to sing:

"I feel like a man awake after long years of sleep. How many did I sleep? . . . I drink up as one long starved this beauty and understanding and joy. . . . I am so happy here — I must belong. . . ." Segesta with its temples — Luxor with its tombs — Naidapur — Singapore — that was the last.

He died there so suddenly, it seems, that there was no time for last words or wishes, but I have always been sure that he wouldn't have wanted to be sent back. He wouldn't have wanted to be changed from his heavy teakwood box and his soft silk pajamas into whatever was nearest to a fashionable mortician's desire. He had gone too far to come back just for a funeral. Yet that is what happened; and since these things the gods allow, I, who don't, had best keep silent.

> Om, Amitaya! Measure not with words
> The immeasurable; nor sink the string of thought
> Into the fathomless. Who asks doth err,
> Who answers errs. Say naught. . . .

# MY
# AUNT PAULINE

"Now THAT the piano has been tuned and had its face washed, don't you want me to straighten out the music for you?"

The young friend who comes sometimes and plays Chopin asked me that the other day and I accepted the offer more gratefully than he could have dreamed. There is so much music here — excess of it, as somebody in Shakespeare said without meaning loose leaves and dusty volumes — and sorting it over now and then is one of the saddest things I do. Even hearing it played again never seems to wake such echoes as I hear when I am silently confronted with its familiar pages. Besides, most of it never is played again, but all of it has to be dusted and straightened out.

I hardly know how so much of it happened to settle down here. Besides my mother's songs and my sister's really good collection brought back from her years in Germany, there are all the " selections " for harp, voice, and piano that register the taste and the ability of my grandmother and my several aunts — my father's sisters. It is interesting that the title pages bear only the names of women, though the men in the family were musical too. I suppose in the South more than elsewhere in their time, both music and " art " were considered feminine accomplishments.

I have to accept almost without reservation the tradition of my aunt Pauline's distinction in both these fields. In addition to the arias and vocalises young Lee has been blowing the dust off of and sorting in neat piles, and my own memories of her voice, there are in the family some admirable portraits, done in the effortless manner that was characteristic of her, to attest the fact that artistic gifts are seldom given singly. I think she might have written too — poetry or romance — besides the delightful letters she did write, and often illustrated with little sketches on the wide margins it was her habit to leave.

I have wished many times that she had at least kept a journal, so that I could have something besides my childish impressions to refer to when I remember some of the things that happened after she married Cousin Gilbert and went to live on his plantation in Mississippi. They were doubtless not so mysterious and enthralling as they seemed, coming to my young ears in the form of folklore, but I still feel that it is a pity to lose them; they might hold their own small candle up to history. They could only have happened as they did because the people in that place and time were as they were.

She was not young when she married, as youth was counted in those days. She was thirty, and so, she said, old enough to know her own mind. Old enough to know better, said the members of the opposition, consisting mainly of brothers. They saw many and grave objections to the step she was taking. Cousin Gilbert was twenty years her senior; he had been married before — if that counted for anything — and was her first cousin, which surely counted for a great deal. One of my uncles, I have since been told, spent a good deal of time searching the Scriptures, with which he was only superficially acquainted, in the hope of finding there his authority for the condemnation of this last ethical infringement.

Cousin Gilbert could hardly have been her only matrimonial temptation, for although she was not considered beautiful, she was graceful and witty (in addition to the accomplishments) and, as her family was now finding out, passionately romantic; but when she gained her point and marriage and the Mississippi plantation closed over her with all of her perfections on her head, she suffered no regrets that I ever heard of — and I listened well. To my restricted childhood my aunt Pauline was what the radio and the cinema are, I suppose, to the wistful young today — life . . . opera . . . art.

The home to which Cousin Gilbert took her after the brief wedding journey was not one of the plantation dwellings of song and story, but it was old and rather sweet, set low in a yard full of jonquils and poets' narcissus. There was a white portico where a coral honeysuckle grew; and inside there was the library with its red curtains and its wood fires, where the tall bookcases had always been and the shining grand piano had come with my aunt Pauline, and where the music, now so dry and dusty, bubbled like a spring. And everywhere of course there were the things left over from Cousin Gilbert's other marriage, reminders of another life and love, by far the most important of which was his little daughter, now in her seventh year.

Nothing sweeter than little Rosa could ever have existed anywhere — not even in Wordsworth — and my aunt Pauline accepted her as the very flower and emblem of romance, a romance that was now her own. The part of her husband's life which she had not shared never seemed to trouble her otherwise than she might have been troubled by a moving story or a play. She had taken everything over, the past as well as the present and the future, by a sort of spiritual *coup d'état* which is perhaps not altogether rare in such cases, and which precluded any whisper of jealousy or suspicion.

I listened, afraid to breathe lest I should be sent upstairs " for a handkerchief " or out to the kitchen to " ask the cook," while she told my mother about the rainy day when she could hear Cousin Gilbert moving about in the room next to hers — the room that had been Rosa's mother's — opening and shutting drawers and putting their contents away. She could hear the rustling of old letters, and then a light metallic sound that must have been her bracelets and jewelry going into his strong-box — " for little Rosa, you know."

" My heart ached for him," she told my mother. " It made me think of *St. Elmo* — you remember. . . ."

My mother remembered; I, alas, could not, for I had never read *St. Elmo*. I did read it — what I could of it — long afterward when it came my way, because I remembered her saying this, and again alas! It has often seemed strange to me, when there is really so little difference between the generations as they come along, that they should make themselves so different in the books they write. I understand my aunt Pauline very well indeed, and my cousin Gilbert too. He was and would be today an agreeable gentleman. St. Elmo, whom they both admired I suppose, is and always was a monster — a Martian.

This was the first time my aunt Pauline had been to see us since her marriage, and her clothes were still new and very elegant, I thought. I was dazzled by the diamond earrings cousin Gilbert had given her. She had had to have her ears pierced so she could wear them, and they had been very long in healing, she told my mother.

"They keep getting hurt all over again. Gilbert says he always seems to be the one. . . ."

"Naturally," said my mother with a smile, and smiled again to see the way the color deepened on the cheek where the bright jewel hung. "Tell me about little Rosa," she went on. "What a lovely child she must be! And what are you planning to do about her education? There are no schools near enough, of course."

"I intend to teach her myself, for the present anyhow," said my aunt with decision. "The governess Gilbert had for her this last year was a dreadful mistake

— a terrible influence for the child. We are just beginning to realize. . . ."

"Did you have to dismiss her," asked my mother, "or was she already gone?"

"She is dead," said my aunt Pauline with a quick glance in my direction, and then began to talk about her garden and how resplendent the roses still were. Jacqueminot . . . Gloire de Dijon . . . long-ago roses that sounded to me like one of her songs.

This was the first of the mysterious allusions to Rosa and her governess that continued to be dropped like pebbles in the limpid depths of my consciousness and send their widening ripples out to embrace a whole new field of knowledge; but a good many years had to pass before I could be considered to have reached the point — to have crossed some imaginary border line — where it would be safe for me to know the "whole story." Again I wish my aunt Pauline had written it, for who shall vouch for it now?

Katie Phelan, the Irish girl, or young lady (any girl who was grown and who was white had a right to the appellation in the South of those days), whom my cousin Gilbert had engaged as a companion for his little daughter, came from a convent school in Gulfport, where she had been educated and had since stayed on as a teacher for the very little children.

She did not like to be called Miss Katie. " I want you all to call me Miss Gertrude," she told the servants, and to little Rosa, who instantaneously adored her, she offered her entire devotion under an astonishing variety of endearing aliases. " Spell it for your Lily, darling; c-a-t; spell it for Désirée. . . ."

This sort of fantastic cajolery acted like a charm on her pupil, who began immediately not only to spell but to read and to memorize everything. The succession of epithets somehow resolved themselves into " Deenie," which may have been a sort of essence or residue of several of them; I do not know. But no name that the future held for Rosa's ears ever fell upon them, I feel sure, with the pure magic of these two foolish syllables. She followed Deenie like a shadow, she hung about her like the air, and Cousin Gilbert, feeling his most anxious problem solved, was entirely content. He must have seen that there was something rather odd about Deenie, but — Irish, convent-bred — what could he expect? . . .

A winter of songs and stories by the nursery grate, where they cracked scaly-barks on the hearth and sometimes cooked exciting things that boiled over on the rug, was succeeded by the sudden onrush of spring; and then Deenie didn't want to stay in the house any more; not even to make up her bed, or Rosa's, or to brush Rosa's curls around the little broomstick she kept in the washstand drawer for the purpose. The beds were left for Delphy, the cook, when she could get around to them some time in the afternoon, and the curls were left to themselves.

Often in the beautiful days that followed one another so closely now, Cousin Gilbert would eat his luncheon quite alone. "They'se done took their'n to the woods with 'em agin," Delphy would say, without criticism but manifestly without approval.

Spring had passed and the summer was passing before a fact that had been common knowledge to others was finally reported to my cousin Gilbert. Deenie and Rosa — his baby! — had been seen almost every day in a boat on the dark sweep of water known as Old River, a part of the yellow Mississippi that had been left behind somehow and was no longer a river but a somber and rather beautiful lake bordered with cypress trees. It was an excellent fishing ground, and the young man who rowed, or punted, the flat-bottomed boat with Deenie and Rosa in it seemed usually on the lookout for a good place to drop his lines. He was a newcomer to that region, whom my cousin Gilbert only knew by sight and of whom he had heard no good whatever.

"So that is who she means by Willy-boy!" He remembered now a name that had been of frequent recurrence in Rosa's chatter, where fact and fantasy had been so commingled of late that he hardly listened any more. How was he to know that Robin Redbreast was the kitten? And now this river-rat who had floated down from God knows where was Willy-boy. . . .

The young man, whose name was really Henry King, lived in a little shack close to the edge of the water from which he drew his living — the legitimate part of it — in the shape of " cat," which he sliced up and sold to the Negroes; and Rosa's father now realized with a flush of anger that she must have been a witness to some spectacular hauls. He had thought she was talking about whales; Jonah maybe. The Bible was included in Deenie's curriculum; not her Bible; his — the " regular one."

He lost no time in sending his plantation manager down to the little fishing shack with a peremptory recommendation to Henry King to leave — to go on down the river, out of the county, out of the state — and he was very much surprised when the young man refused to do so. He wasn't on anybody's land, he argued with some show of logic; how could anybody order him to get off of it?

Deenie of course was forbidden to set foot outside of the yard where the jonquils and the narcissus had long since bloomed and faded and where the Michaelmas daisies were opening their soberer eyes. These were orders that my cousin Gilbert had more right to issue and could with vigilance enforce — up to a certain point; but Deenie, poor foolish Deenie, found a way to nullify them of which he had not even dreamed.

It seemed a heavenly interposition that sent Delphy into her room to waken her before Rosa had gone in and found her there, so plainly not asleep. There was no bottle anywhere, no glass; but the doctor said it was poison of some kind, laudanum maybe — from her eyes. He was a country doctor, but, after all, what difference did it make? There was a reason — a very natural reason according to the ethics of those days, and one which the dresses of those days had enabled her to conceal — why she did not want to live.

All the finalities were hurried on account of Rosa. Deenie had no parents, and the relative who had paid for her tuition at the convent could not be located. No friends appeared to ask questions or make delays. In the shortest possible time everything was over.

What lies were told the child by the servants, by her father himself in his desperate wish to hide from her all aspects of the tragedy, it would be hard to say — or which of them she believed. Even the least unusual children have a curious faculty for dealing with fatalities, and Rosa was not one of these. But at any rate it was very shortly after this that my aunt Pauline arrived in the

theater of her life, to play there her leading and benefi-
cent role and to rectify as immediately as might be the
unfortunate results of poor Deenie's blundering passage.

How many times she asked herself what did Rosa
know, what had she seen, of all that must have preceded
the wretched ending? Those many hours in the boat;
those other hours — where? She was soon convinced,
however, that whatever Rosa knew an angel might have
known without ruffling a feather. What she had seen
was of course another matter.

My aunt Pauline's visits to us at this time were of the
briefest nature. She came only when shopping or other
necessary matters brought her up to Memphis (it was
more of a journey in those days) and she seemed to be
always anxious about what might be happening in her
absence. She had Rosa continually in her thoughts.

"The most important thing I have to do," she said to
my mother, "is to teach her to distinguish between what
is real and what she only imagines. There is no way that
I know of to make her understand that Deenie is dead,
but I ought to be able to make her realize that she is not
there any longer. Rosa believes she sees her; she talks
to her, and even tells me sometimes what Deenie says."

"What does she say?" my mother not unnaturally
inquired.

"Foolishness. Always the most absurd things. If I

were to repeat them you would think the child was delirious, or bewitched. But she is really quite normal about other things. She is very healthy, and I should say unusually bright."

" Of course she is," said my mother reassuringly. " Her imagination has just been overstimulated; that is all. Children always outgrow these fancies. You must give her time."

The shadow on my aunt's thoughtful face did not lift. " There is something else," she said. " Perhaps I should not speak of it, but I cannot help feeling that that poor girl's death ought to have been looked into a little more. Everything was done so hurriedly. Nobody seemed to be thinking of her at all; only of Rosa."

" But wasn't it a clear case of suicide? "

" It doesn't seem so clear to me any longer; not since I have learned so much more about her — how gay she was, and all that nonsense she carried on. I don't know why it is so appealing. I just can't make myself believe she drank that stuff — whatever it was — on purpose."

" But she did drink it? "

" Maybe she thought it was something else. Maybe that miserable man had something to do with it."

" Where is he now? " asked my mother. " I mean, where did he go? "

My aunt hesitated for a moment. " He is still there," she said. " Off and on, that is. He keeps coming back."

She was confronted, it now appeared, by a new anxiety; she was afraid that Cousin Gilbert might resort to means which were at any time within his reach, but of which she disapproved, to rid the country permanently of the presence of Henry King. There would be annoyances — scandal, maybe.

" I don't see why he insists so on staying. There must be plenty of catfish farther down the river. He even talks to the servants whenever he meets them anywhere off of the place. Delphy told me the other day he stopped her on the way home and asked her if she wasn't going to bring ' little Missy ' down to Old River again some time. The idea! I haven't even dared to tell Gilbert. Maybe it isn't true. They are such liars — even Delphy."

But this time, it seemed, Delphy had told the truth. For some reason Henry King was trying to see Rosa again, and when my aunt returned to the plantation, the first thing she learned was that he had succeeded.

He had managed to approach the house unseen and speak to Rosa, who was playing in the yard. Her father was, as usual at that time of the morning, out somewhere on the plantation, and nobody ever did know where Delphy and the others were, but certainly not within sight or hearing of " little Missy."

The child was both candid and casual about Willy-boy's visit. Indeed they only knew he had been there because she told them.

" What did he say to you, Rosa? " her father asked.

" Oh, we talked about fishing," answered Rosa, " and he told me to find the money for him."

" The money, darling? "

" He said Deenie told him for me to find it and then he would come and get it. On tomorrow, he said."

This rendezvous, needless to say, was never kept. Before tomorrow dawned, Willy-boy was on his way downstream, and this time, fortunately for him, he did not return. But Rosa continued to expect him and still talked of finding Deenie's money. And then one day she did.

" Here it is," she announced, bringing a small inlaid box to my aunt Pauline. There was more than a hundred dollars in it — almost all the money Cousin Gilbert had paid her. There were some little bits of jewelry too, and a silver medal and a lock of hair.

" Where did you find it, darling? "

" In the closet where the shoeses dance."

" Who told you it was there? " (But why ask that?) " Did Deenie tell you to go look in the closet? "

"She just kept saying: 'In the closet where the little shoeses dance all night.' There is a hole down in the floor. The shoeses danced it there."

One could wish that the story ended at this point; but the hole in the closet floor, which was really there and had doubtless been made the subject of elfin imaginings between Deenie and Rosa, contained something else that Rosa had not found. Under the little square of board that had been patched and had come loose again there was room not only for the hidden treasure but for a bottle almost full of some dark liquid — the bottle about which they had all wondered.

It bore a label setting forth the virtues of its contents as a very present help in a kind of trouble that even the "young ladies" of those conservative days had sometimes to cope with, it would seem, for Mother Watkins' Tonic, as the stuff was called, was a popular nostrum, easily procurable even in rural districts, and Henry King, having procured it, found it equally easy to remove the cork and fortify its comparatively harmless and by no means certain potentialities with ingredients known to be sure. Deenie had taken only a very little, but it was quite enough.

These conjectures, which were accepted so immediately as facts that, in a manner of speaking, they became so, still left several things to be explained — besides the central mystery of Rosa's apparent traffic with the spirit world, which was never fathomed to anybody's satisfaction and which, as my mother had predicted, soon ceased to be an influence in her life.

It is impossible not to ask, for one thing, why Henry King should have taken this way of removing Deenie and any trouble she might cause him, when it would have been so easy for him just to drop down the river and not return. But perhaps we should ask why death is always so apt to take a hand in affairs of this nature. One has only to read the morning paper — any paper on almost any one of our more enlightened mornings — to see how he still keeps his agents ready.

Then, too, Willy-boy very plainly did not want to move. He had his vested interests there, his boat, his shack, and his associates. Why should he go just because he was asked to? He had never in his life perhaps been asked to stay anywhere.

The money, Deenie's little hoard, I am inclined to think only came into his plans later on, when he had probably learned by talking to the servants that the family was unaware of its existence. He doubtless knew about it from Deenie, and thought, not without reason, that he might get his hands on it by means of Rosa.

As I have said, he never came back nor, so far as I know, was he ever heard of again. Even no longer ago than that we did not make the determined effort we make today to recover those social units known as good riddances. They were many times permitted just to drop out of the story, which besides saving trouble in other ways was likely to make a nicer ending for the story.

"I often think we should worship the river the way the Egyptians did the Nile, instead of just fearing it; it sweeps away so many obnoxious things. . . ." I seem to hear again the lovely tones of my aunt Pauline consigning the derelict to his deserved oblivion.

# FOOD AND DRUGS

I WONDER if all big places in the country seem to offer such a field for experiment in the arts and crafts as this one has always done — especially to the young. Our more youthful friends have undertaken to do things here that I am sure they would never have thought of doing anywhere else. They have given rein to their hobbies and unleashed their untried talents without restriction among us. What a place to write in — to paint in — to weave rugs in! . . . How often have we heard it and how often smiled!

Fortunately the walls are thick and the ceilings high, and anyone practicing the flageolet downstairs has never had to annoy anyone else adapting a pageant upstairs, or inventing a new dish in the kitchen, or making wine in the cellar.

It was seeing the vaulted roof of the cellar one day when he went down there with Mary to get a jar of preserves that inspired our young friend William to experiment with the grape, and the æsthetic masonry overhead continued to console him in some measure for more dampness than he expected underfoot. He soon disclosed an unmistakable gift for the manufacture of vintages and read up on the subject enough to learn at least in part why his wine was so much better than anybody thought it was going to be.

From this venture more benefits have flowed than from most of the enthusiasms that have swept over us. William was not even allowed to drop it after the customary interval. He was encouraged from every side to keep it up by offers of help in the parts of the process that required the least virtuosity, such as " shucking " the grapes from the bunches or washing the bottles.

I do not know who may remember the bottles, but I for one will not forget those golden October week-ends when we would sit around the big stone table under the pecan tree up to our elbows in purple juice, helping

William shuck. We would eat all the best ones and throw the worst ones to the peacocks, who never failed to join us, and put the others into big stone crocks to be mashed with the potato masher; and in spite of all this amateurish procedure the wine was really professional. It could only be called homemade because it was and not because it tasted so. Why don't people who live in the country always make wine in the autumn, as a crowning gesture to the fruitful year? Because not many men have time for it I suppose, and women — why don't women do a lot of things?

The old saying that the way to a man's heart is through his stomach should be amended, it seems to me — lifted gastronomically to admit the idea of preparing food as well as consuming it. I have known few men in my life who didn't love to cook, and I believe they were only the ones who had never tried it. It has long been a mystery to me how the kitchens of the world ever got into the hands of women.

One Christmas we gave Randolph, who had something of a reputation to maintain in this field, the *Delmonico Cook Book* (illustrated), which is probably the biggest cook book in the world, being about the size of the family Bible, with much the same gilt and morocco dignity. We found it in a rare-book shop, and since it was not too expensive for a joke, we thought it would be rather a good one. But it turned out to be serious. Not only Randolph but every male visitor who came to the house that Christmas fell completely under the spell of those trussed fowls and *meringues glacées.* One after another at various times they would pick up the book and open its pages and be heard to speak no more, even when spoken to. There was something rather Freudian about it — some sort of suppressed desire or wish-fulfillment.

Before the holidays were over, the Delmonico atmosphere was precipitated into a dinner party for which each of the initiates executed one of the dishes. The most ambitious of these, as I recall it, was a *coq en pâte,* in which the bird, hermetically sealed in pastry, was supposed to retain the last drop of its essence and reach the palate in a distillation of unparalleled strength and purity. It was considered a success, I believe, in spite of some murmurings about " more gravy," and the *bombe au chocolat,* for which a mold had to be borrowed from the Peabody Hotel, was so spectacular, borne in on a silver platter with its fuse lighted, that nobody liked to mention a spot of brine that had somehow leaked in.

This was one dinner party that seems to me to have been given in the right spirit, for the food alone; with the nose in the trough as it were. All the others to which I have been invited were given for something else, and the food, however exquisite or however poor, was equally unmentioned. Nobody goes to concerts like that, or to plays or picture galleries. A delicious dish is a great achievement and should be applauded, and a bad one should be hooted at — unless, of course, it is an accident, like the salt in the ice cream — and opinions should be freely expressed. *De gustibus,* etc., is all very well, but if such matters are not to be discussed, how are they to be uplifted or rectified? There is nearly always a chance, even after a dish has come to the table, of putting something into it that may improve it, however little there may be of taking anything out.

My mother, who always asked people to " stay to lunch " and then slipped out to the kitchen and went to " no trouble at all " to see that things were a little dressier than usual (the cream whipped for the chocolate though we liked it better plain, and the cold chicken made into croquettes though our favorite phase of a waning fowl was hash), was once entertaining a country neighbor in this impromptu fashion and feeling rather pleased that Miss Letty had dropped in on a day when the lunch was better than usual, only to have her spirits dashed by a remark Miss Letty made after it was over, as she sat ruminating by the parlor fire.

" You all don't use black pepper, do you? " she said, not critically, only reflectively, but, alas, too late.

I have seen it stated that in grading the world's cooks the Chinese and the French are so far in the lead that it doesn't matter where you put the others. I have thought for a long while that our national cuisine would rank pretty low. Even Southern cooking, so much esteemed at its best, is so often at its worst that the tradition suffers. We all have our noble recipes, handed down from the brave days when we took — when somebody took — " two dozen eggs and a gallon of rich cream " . . . but the miracles performed with these ingredients have fallen back into the past as far almost as the loaves and fishes. Those of us who still believe in them could not do better than to try, within our restricted scope — our gills and ounces — to get them out of the windy hall of fame and back into the kitchen.

In our own family we have, I am proud to say, one hereditary masterpiece that continues to be made by somebody whenever Christmas rolls round: a baronial survival known as a " spiced round of beef." I do not know where the original recipe came from; I have never found it in any cook book that came my way; but it should not be allowed to perish from the earth.

The first person I ever saw make it was my Nashville grandmother, and I remember how far away Christmas still seemed when she began on it. I remember her long colloquies with the butcher about the size and shape and boning of the beef — all things that must be settled to her satisfaction, and settled early so there would still be time enough for pickling " in slow brine " (as Cleopatra said in giving a formula for something else) before the really enchanting steps could be taken: the larding and spicing and pressing, and finally the cooking and cooling and slicing paper-thin for supper on Christmas night.

One who has never followed through from the beginning such a culinary achievement will always have, it seems to me, a gap in his mentality and should not be allowed a voice (which can never be other than a tinkling cymbal) on the subject of preparing food.

I not only watched my grandmother do these things; I helped. " *Pars magna fui,*" I might have said with Virgil, had I known him at the time. I remember especially being the one chosen to take the cinnamon and cloves and mace and nutmeg around to the neighboring drugstore and wait while the obliging druggist pounded them in his stone mortar with his stone pestle. I still look forward to the day when I am going to own a mortar and pestle. Of course we can now shake all the spices of Arabia through the perforated top of a tin can, but something in me makes me want to buy my cinnamon in sticks and my pepper in " corns " and grate my fingers along with my nutmeg.

## FOOD AND DRUGS

There was something dim and mysterious about that drugstore — about all drugstores when I was a child. One would like to speak of them as " chemist shops," or " the apothecary's," to differentiate them — since they were so different — from those centers of frivolity we have today, flowing with beverages, flaming with magazines, crackling with celophane. . . .

Somebody writing about Keats once suggested that the " lucent syrops, tinct with cinnamon," and other confections he describes in *The Eve of Saint Agnes* were a mental flash-back to his own handling of such articles in the days when he was a chemist's assistant. I am sure that children who cannot remember the big red and green bottles in the drugstore windows have missed one early influence that they ought to have. One might write an " Ode on the Atmosphere of Pharmacy," and had better do it soon or nobody will know what it is about.

I remember going into a drugstore in a little town in Italy where all such rich associations as I have in mind were quite undissipated; Romeo might have been there shouting: " What ho, apothecary! " instead of me inquiring for toothpaste. I was almost ashamed to do it, face to face with all those mysterious-looking pots and jars, and felt as if I ought to ask the bearded druggist for henbane or mandragora or some other " such soon-speeding gear " that I had no use for but that seemed more likely to be there.

It is strange, when we hear so much these days about raw materials, and the nations are pouring out their blood like water to get hold of them, that there are more and more people all the time living out their lives contentedly without ever having seen one. They never even see them in bulk any more, or loose, or any way except in packages — smaller and smaller packages. Pretty soon there will not be one in any grocery or drugstore that is too big to swallow whole; the trend of civilization has set definitely toward pills and capsules.

But even a capsule can be swallowed with more interest if one has ever tasted or smelled, or even seen, the stuff inside of it, if only to know what one is being spared. It is not the comfort of the arrangement I am considering, but its imaginative restrictions. Take quinine for instance. Hundreds of grains of it are consumed every year in this part of the world by people who have no conception of what it is they are taking — of how bitter it is, or how beautiful — having never seen it shaken out of a big blue bottle, as I used to see my father do it, onto a white sheet of paper that always ceased to be white and turned into a dingy yellow under that light fall of snow. Nothing I have ever seen is as white or as soft as quinine, and my father would sit for a half-hour

or so at the table after breakfast cramming it into capsules and " measuring out " on his knife blade the calo-
mel to be taken with it and folding it into little squares
of paper.

Those were the days when chills and fever were accepted more broad-mindedly than they are today as a
part of human experience, and my father maintained a
sort of free dispensary for his country neighbors (mostly
black), being at the same time very bountiful where his
family was concerned. Nobody thought it strange that,
though a lawyer by profession, he should know " all
about " medicine too, and his prescriptions were swallowed without question by young and old — nature
alone protesting when the knife blade may have come
up too heavily laden from the mercurial bottle or the
capsule have been too conscientiously packed.

The expense of this purely personal charity must have
been considerable, taken year in, year out, and my father
always stocked his shelves with wholesale sizes of everything. It may be that seeing the dark bottles with their
insignia of skull and crossbones standing beside the
crystal pints of glycerine and camphor in the bathroom
closet would have for children even now the charm it
had for me.

But it was an arrangement that had its perils too, and
when putting up nocturnal prescriptions hastily called

for, it would no doubt have been safer to have had the more lethal bottles standing in a place by themselves; for that was before the days of rural electricity, and my father, who said it always took so long to light a lamp, never hesitated to dispense a remedy by the light of a match or even of the moon. Fortunately his eyesight was phenomenal and only once that I know of did he make a mistake and send something meant for paregoric but very far from being it to old Uncle Peter, suffering the midnight consequences of a catfish and buttermilk supper. Even then the Lord was on both their sides for the little darky who had run half a mile clutching the bottle to get the medicine fell and broke it in running the half-mile back, and Uncle Peter, who never knew that it had contained a sure ticket over Jordan, managed to pull through without it, still on the hither shore.

There were hazards in my father's therapy, and in my grandmother's cooking too, no doubt. When we begin operations on the hoof so to speak, the range of possible mistakes is naturally increased; but the glory of successful achievement is undoubtedly greater, or undoubtedly seems to be; and even in the case of failure, there is so much more in the longer formula that one can lay it on. There is always the pleasure of the post-mortem, when one can wander back almost indefinitely from effect to cause: the cake that looked so good and wasn't because we could taste the butter that was churned from the cream that was milked from the cow that fed on the onions that Jack planted. . . . Whereas if one makes a failure nowadays, with everything pre-tested, pre-measured, and pre-mixed, there is no longer anything to blame for it. Perhaps it might be argued that there are no longer any failures; but there again, isn't there something rather tasteless about too much success?

OCCULT

I HAVE BEEN watching Jubby, stretched out on his side in front of the fire and dreaming of the chase. I woke him up finally, because running rabbits in profile that way is hard on the rug, and his sobs when they get away from him fairly rend my heart. Anyway I don't like to be reminded of what futile things dreams are, when we put so much into them. Jubby was putting everything he had, except perhaps good sense, into that dream: desire and hope and anguish, besides actual physical energy, and it seemed to me he ought to have something to show for it — not a rabbit exactly, but something. I knew of course he wouldn't, so I woke him up. Perhaps I shouldn't have, for he is still looking at me reproachfully. He probably thinks now it was my fault the rabbit got away.

There have always been people who claimed that they did get something out of their dreams. Coleridge, for instance, certainly caught his rabbit if he wrote *Kubla Khan* in his sleep. But I didn't know Coleridge, and if the people I do know have ever reaped a material benefit from a dream, it has never been reported to me in anything like a convincing fashion.

We all know that dreams are endlessly interesting, and if we have been reading books on the new time-theories, we probably know that we have been mistaken about their real place in our experience. I am one of Mr. J. W. Dunne's followers — in so far as one can follow Mr. Dunne without equations. Fortunately, I was able to accept a good deal of his theory before he set out to prove it mathematically, and I am permanently convinced that we dream about future events quite as readily, if not quite so often, as we do about past ones. Even this cannot be called a practical benefit, however, if we have to blunder through the events in exactly the same way. So, at least, it seems to me — though maybe the equations might help me there.

I have always been interested in things seen through psychic keyholes and behind lifted veils and the like, and very favorably disposed toward any glimmerings we can get from other planes, but I have ceased to hope that they will ever give us the kind of light we need to walk by on this one. Roberta and her apparitions; Clarke and his intimations — what end is ever gained, what doom averted, by these rare and favored glimpses (even if we accept them) into an outlying scheme that fails to correspond with ours? I suppose I could say that Deenie gave little Rosa a practical hint about where to find the bottle, but I dare say she had already suggested a hundred other hiding places. . . .

The best thing about psychic experiences, I think, is the fun we get out of telling them afterward. Everybody likes to talk about the supernatural adventures that have come his way, first-, second-, or third-hand, and occasionally somebody even likes to listen. My favorite contribution to this form of entertainment is the story of Gloria, who was, I believe, the only disinterested medium I ever knew and certainly the only one I ever lived in the same house with.

Gloria came to us direct from Porto Fino, in answer to an advertisement I had put in an Italian paper — not for a medium, but for a cook. She represents, up to the present, my one effort to escape from the toils of my bondage to the colored servants who fill my life with mirth and misery down here in Dixie, and who were filling it just then to running over. Somewhere in the broad universe, I had cried, there must be something for me different from this; and Gloria was what I got.

She made the long voyage very inexpensively on a tramp steamer, and at New Orleans was put aboard the train by a clerk from the consul's office. In Memphis we met her at the depot and brought her home. All very simple.

She was a good-looking girl of the rugged peasant type, and spoke rather good Italian in addition to her rugged peasant dialect, and we settled down at once to learn about her all the things we had to know.

The first of these was that as a servant she was without an equal in our experience. She could do practically everything and do it well, and when it was all done, she would sit down and embroider table napkins. I believe her psychic gifts were almost the last thing we found out about her. It happened this way:

One morning I went upstairs, where she had been dusting the bedrooms, and on the hall table by the telephone I noticed an odd little picture, sketched with a pencil on a leaf from the tablet I kept there to write addresses in. It was not particularly well done, though far better than anything I could have done myself; but the subject struck me immediately as being like an illustration for the detective story our young friend David had been reading aloud to us the evening before. I took it downstairs with me when I went and laid it before him.

" Did you do this? " I asked.

" I did not," he answered. " Where did you get it? "

That was the beginning of a pretty spirited investigation. I don't know why we were so long in asking Gloria about the sketch, but when we did she admitted quite simply that she had drawn it. She had drawn such pictures many times, she said. Sometimes they were pictures of things that had happened and sometimes the things didn't happen until afterward. She had drawn the Pope on his death-bed before even the doctors knew he was going to die. Father Paolo had kept it and put it in a little frame. Everyone in Porto Fino knew about the pictures she drew. . . .

I asked her what this one was about and she said she didn't know. I asked her where she had been sitting or standing, whether she was awake or asleep when she drew it, and she didn't know these things either; but when I suggested that she do another one for me, she seemed quite shocked. " Oh no, signora, it only comes when God wills it," she said. Then she laid the picture down and began to talk about the *frittura* of chicken I had " commanded " for dinner.

We were having a lot of company that fall — mostly young — and I was sorry (though of course it was inevitable) to have them find out about Gloria's psychic gift and behave as they did about it. I thought it was too bad, when she was making them all so comfortable, for them to go around thinking of her as one possessed. The fact that she couldn't understand what they said about her made them feel they never had to drop the subject as we generally have to when the servants come in, and it was positively childish, the way they would go into the rooms after she had made them so beautifully neat and muss everything up again, hoping to find the next picture. David was the worst, as well as the most hopeful, and felt fully justified when he was the one to find it. Being one of the boys who likes to cook, he had gone into the kitchen while she was out of it, to " toss up a pound cake," and when he pushed the bread-box out of the way, there it was. She had drawn it on quite a large piece of paper this time — the kind we use for the kitchen shelves — with the pencil she kept to make out her laborious grocery lists.

It was decidedly surrealist in conception. There was a tower led up to by several flights of narrow and precipitous steps. A man was going up the steps, and some

small objects that might have been either birds or brick-
bats were falling (or flying) around his head. Another
figure, very anatomical and sinewy, was lying prone in
the right-hand corner of the picture, with a stream of
blood gushing from its heart; and over the whole
sketch she had drawn a very intricate web with a long-
legged spider in the middle of it. It was all quite clear,
though its meaning naturally was not; and very well
done for anybody who couldn't — or at least wouldn't
— draw at all when she was in her normal state of mind.

"How's that for a menace?" David said, smoothing
the picture out on the table for us to see.

It was really an extraordinary group of images, exactly like the makings of a dream, and I was sure that
for Gloria it had been just that — one of those dreams
we forget immediately on waking and never have to
account for. But she had been led by her strange gift to
make it visible, and we were all trying to account for
it as hard as ever we could.

We talked about it all through luncheon, and of course
got our biggest thrill in assuming it was a dire predic-
tion for somebody. "To know Cassandra was to know
the worst," David quoted cheerfully; but when I saw
him later in the afternoon getting out his tennis racket,
I had an idea of my own.

"Is Constance taking you on again this afternoon?"

I asked him. " Better have another look at the picture. That might be a tennis net instead of a web; and Constance has nice long arms and legs, you know. Marvelous at catching things. . . ."

" Now, you lay off Constance," David said. " Her intentions aren't nearly as honorable as you think they are."

But he did take another look at the picture.

On Saturday William came out with six bushels of grapes in his car and began to look things over in the cellar and get ready for a vinous week-end. The wine-press (really a cider-press) was set up on the back porch, and pretty soon the call went out for volunteers to help in the grape-shucking, and everybody began to gather round.

William had gone back into the cellar. When he came up the steep little stairs again, he was greeted with cheers, for he was bringing two bottles of his proudest vintage — his sparkling Burgundy — to inaugurate the autumn festival. The applause must have made him forget the step with the nick of cement broken out of it, for he caught his foot on it and pitched forward on the stone floor of the porch, full length, in a red river of wine. He was up in an instant, quite unhurt, but everybody had remembered the picture.

" The face on the bar-room floor! " Mary cried. " You are the one Cassandra is gunning for. Either she thinks you oughtn't to be making wine or she doesn't like the kind you make. Anyhow, you had better quit it. . . ."

William laughed obligingly at the joke, and Joe mopped him off and brought him one of his house aprons to put on, and out by the stone table things proceeded as usual, but without the ceremonial wine.

" Do you suppose," Mary whispered to David as she leaned over to take a bunch from his basket, " that he really is a little scared? "

" A little Scotch," he whispered back.

The picture had begun to lose some of its interest by the time the week-enders dispersed, which was not a bad thing for most of us. It was going to be a busy week for me. This was the time of year to remember about the autumn rains, and that some of the chimneys were full of soot and all the gutters full of leaves. The Negro bricklayer whom we always have for jobs within his scope, and who had the requisite ladders for this one, had been engaged to come. While he was on the roof I meant to have him repair the corner of the tower where the lightning had struck it some years before in one of our spectacular thunderstorms.

I awoke on Monday morning to the sound of footsteps

on the slate and ladders being dragged and lifted to the different levels, accompanied by voices loud and gay; and by the time I came down to breakfast, Tom Green and his assistants were in full possession of the premises.

So much has been said in appreciation of Negroes singing at their work that we have come to consider it their privilege to do so, no matter where they happen to be working, but it is harder to appreciate their long-distance conversations. Jokes cracked on the roof and guffawed at from the basement seem to me inconsiderate in the early hours of the morning; but I have never suggested, and never heard of anyone suggesting, to Negro workmen that less noise would be acceptable, or even possible. Maybe it isn't. Certainly the young giant scraping the mortar-bed with his hoe in the back yard was determined not to miss anything being said on the tower as he sent his buckets back and forth along the rope that had been stretched for them. " Say which? " he would bawl, his face upturned expectantly, and everything would have to be repeated for his benefit.

It was in the afternoon of the second day of this, and I was counting the hours to quitting-time and the silence that would fall once more, when I realized it had suddenly fallen. No scraping or pounding, all at once — no voices, high or low. It was rather startling and I hurried out into the yard and looked up. There was no one on the tower. The ladders were still there, but the rope hung motionless and slack. I went around where the mortar-bed was located, thinking I would find my workmen taking simultaneous naps, and there I did find them, but not asleep. The two bricklayers were bending over the other man, who was sitting on a pile of bricks, holding his head forward so that the blood which was running down his face would drip on the ground and not on his open undershirt.

It was only a little cut on the side of his nose made by a sharp fragment of brick that must have fallen from pretty high up while he was watching his friends on the tower, but there was something almost fatal about the scene as I came upon it: the steady drip into the little pool of blood that was forming already at his feet, his attitude of quiet waiting, and the complete silence into which all three of the men had fallen. . . .

I cannot remember which was first of all the many things we tried in our effort to check those persistent drops. Everybody on the place appeared with remedies and suggestions: hot water, ice water, cotton and tissue paper, iodine and alum; and of course we were all the time telephoning for a doctor and meeting with all the inevitable delays. Still he kept that dying-gladiator pose, refusing to lie down or to be moved in any way, least of all in the direction of a hospital (his own pappy had died in one, he said), and the pool, which was a little river now, began running toward the sea.

I felt almost as if I couldn't bear it. It seemed so unnatural for anyone with all that vital fluid in him just to sit there patiently and give it up. I had gone into the kitchen for something and was staying there until I could stop crying, when Aunt Althea came in. She had run all the way from her cabin over in the far corner of Mr. Weakley's field (such is the efficacy of the " grapevine ") to ask us why in the name of Gawd we didn't put some spider-web on the cut so's it would stop bleedin'. . . .

I still smile — I had to even then — at the way everybody, winged with this new hope, began flying in every direction in search of cobwebs. Normally the most inevitable of nuisances, they now became for some reason rare and elusive. My own choice of a hunting ground was the garden, where I am always getting them in my eyes and in my hair, but that of course is in the twilight (*araignée du soir*) and now the sun was shining. Some of the others went under the beds and sofas, seeking in vain what nobody ever failed to find before; but the combined total of our collected wisps proved to be sufficient, for it worked — something did.

It is true the patient had been obliged to lie down just as Aunt Althea blanketed his nose — suddenly, with his head on a brick, because he had fainted — and the doubting may say, if they like, that it was this change in his position that stopped the hemorrhage, but there were no doubters among us then. We knew it was Gloria's picture. . . .

We have the picture still, but we did not have Gloria very much longer. Before the spirit moved her to draw another one, the tramp steamer on which she had arrived made its round trip back and she broke the news to us that she was pledged to return on it — pledged to the first mate. It seemed that on that halcyon freighter coming over, there had been time enough for anything and Gloria had put it to the uses of romance.

I hated to lose my cook; I rather hated to lose my medium, for in those days I was still hopeful of astral advantages. But to have a cook and a medium at the same time, one should really have two people. Combining them would be sure to precipitate something sooner or later and be bad for the psyche — or even for the digestion.

# ÆSTHETIC

I AM SOMETIMES asked by lovely ladies to read my verses before their various literary " groups," and the time may come when, in conformity with the role of ageing poetess, I shall begin to accept such invitations — if they are still extended. I shall then no doubt consider it either a duty or a pleasure to do so. I wonder which.

It was really both that led me to address the " Dilettantes " on the poetry of Rainer Maria Rilke and to read some translations from his *Stundenbuch* which I had made for an American review a short while before.

At that time I was the only person in this country,

as far as I could ascertain, who had ever heard of Rilke. He seemed to have swum into my ken alone, and I felt that I must spread his gospel through all the avenues open to me. This was one, and I besought my audience of smart and intelligent women not to stop with anything I had written or could say about his poetry, but to seek its beauty where it might be found. There were no takers, however, for the little volumes I had brought along to tempt them. Few had any German; none had any time; they just thought it was perfectly lovely and went home.

Rilke has come into his own since then, in this as in other lands, but I fear the Dilettantes have never heard of him again.

I was spending the winter in Geneva, providing a background for Mary and some of her young friends, when his books first fell into my hands. If I had known how short a time on earth remained to him, I think perhaps I might have made an effort to meet him. He was not very far away just then — at the Château de Muzot.

As it was, I only wrote to him, sending him the few translations I had made and asking him, in the interest of the paper I proposed to write, for some slight biographical notes, since I could find so little about him published anywhere.

The letter I had from him in reply was charming, and

while he withheld the data I had requested and gave his reasons for always declining to make this sort of direct appearance, he sent me a book which I am sure he meant me to take in part at least as biographical.

This letter, the only one I ever had from him, now fills its small place in his *Collected Correspondence*. The book, with its priceless inscription, I found this spring fallen behind some larger books and made into confetti by an industrious mouse. No other book had ever to my knowledge been treated like this before. Why did such a treasure have to be singled out for destruction?

The mouse was no doubt happily concerned with the cheap German paper, so quickly reduced to the little heap before me, while I, remembering the ordered procession of words — the gardens and palaces of thought — felt as if I were looking on the ruins of some Cambodian city.

David, who was a dilettante in all but the club sense and who had a great deal more time than those alert housewives and mothers to follow the far trails, gave Rilke a very different welcome; nor was he going to let a little thing like the German language stand between them long. He was good at languages and was soon leaping this and other hurdles on his way to a complete appreciation of the poet.

" Just listen to this," he would call from the shadiest window in the coolest room, to whoever happened to be passing, in the heat and in a hurry:

> " Die Landschaft, wie ein Vers im Psalter,
> Ist Ernst und Wucht und Ewigkeit —

Hotcha! "

All the same we were surprised, though we should not have been, knowing he was in the front of the little-theater movement, when he announced one day that he was going to do " something dramatic " with Rilke. " I think I shall make a short play of *The Love and Death of Cornet Christophe.* We can put it on out of doors."

Where out of doors? we asked him. How would he manage about the different scenes?

That, he said, was the best thing he was going to do — something entirely original. He would not move the scenery; he would move the audience. " The first scene, where Christophe and the others are on horseback, will be in the woods . . . bright armor among the trees. . . ."

" Real horses? "

" Why not? We can use our two as far as they will go and borrow the rest — from the neighbors or from the Polo Club. A free ticket for anybody who furnishes a horse." Somebody suggested "horse-play," but David was not listening. "Let me see—that scene begins: 'The young von Langenau turned in his saddle,' and goes on to the bivouac by the wayside shrine. We can have a live Madonna. Who is the blondest of the gals we know?"

It began to sound interesting and we let him go on to describe the scene in the garden: "And then the next one, up in the Gräfin's chamber—well, of course we couldn't have that one anyhow. It will just have to be indicated."

Somebody asked him how they did asterisks on the stage, but he paid no attention to that either; he was in earnest and we realized it when we saw him beginning to tone his conception down and bring it within the range of an actual performance. He gave up the idea of a cavalcade. That would be more shining armor than even he felt up to, so he mounted two of his officers and left the rest on foot. He was astonishingly adroit about the whole business, and the wayside shrine was a triumph of venerable architecture by the time he got through with it. Knocked together by a country carpenter and painted a pristine white, it had aged under his hands and under our very eyes into the counterpart of crumbling stone. He had stripped the moss off the north side of something and stuck it on somehow where it would be most effective, and one could see already how the flaxen Louise would look standing stiffly in her niche, in a dim blue dress, with the summer woods behind her.

My contribution to the properties was to be the banner that makes so important a figure in the brief story, and I had lavishly decided to cut up into three lengths a roll of heavy Chinese brocade in a beautiful and unreal shade of red which had been sent to me years before by one of the navy members of the family. A pikestaff tipped with gold and a wide golden fringe — and behold a *Fahne* like a sunset flame. It seemed worth the sacrifice.

I finished it on the Saturday afternoon before the play was to come off. We had decided to have it on Sunday because there was quite a solemn feeling in the air about all this beauty we seemed to ourselves to be creating. David wanted to put " at the hour of Vespers " on the highly selective invitations he was getting out, but somebody reminded him of the Gräfin's chamber and he put six o'clock instead.

We had all of us put a lot into the thing, first and last. Louise had practiced her Byzantine expression until it had become almost a fixture, and everybody practiced his lines incessantly, in English, and in German too when he could. The one I seemed to be hearing most of the time was the one that proclaims in the last scene the absence of the flag:

*Aber die Fahne war nicht dabei. . . .*

They said it and they sang it, and in the light of the discovery we made on Sunday morning when we began assembling the properties, the words were prophetic.

Everything had been left out on the porch, heaped on chairs and tables, so we could get at it more conveniently when the time came to set the scenes, and the flag was there with the rest; we had all seen it standing in the corner, carefully furled about its tall pole, late Saturday evening after the dress rehearsal; then on Sunday when we looked for it, it had disappeared.

It was of course useless to ask the servants, and this time it even seemed unreasonable to suspect them — though we did both. Every one of them had been there all the time, and working like mad in the interests of the play; they had even given up their Sunday off and seemed just as anxious to make it a success as we were.

We wasted so much time looking for and bemoaning the lost banner that there was very little left in which to devise a substitute when we finally had to. But we did the best we could with a shawl and a mop-handle and consoled ourselves after the manner of amateurs by saying the audience wouldn't know the difference.

The sun lent its level shafts of light in a most co-operative fashion to illuminate the forest glimpses where " the young von Langenau turned in his saddle," and by the time the scene in the garden began, the mystery of twilight which we had invoked by careful timing was doing what it could to veil sundry deficiences about which we had been able to do nothing.

Real darkness came on for the fire and flight of the final spectacle, and the indirect lighting from the various colored combustibles around the corner of the house, to which David now applied a fuse, threw a highly creditable reflection of flame over the " courtyard." The two dear horses, who didn't like it, plunged about with an ad lib. artistry that helped out the idea of a stampede beyond our brightest hopes, and when the hoofbeats ceased and the last flicker was extinguished and the contrasting night and silence fell for the final curtain, we felt that Rilke himself might have liked it. . . . *Aber die Fahne war nicht dabei.* . . .

But on Monday morning, there it was, standing in its corner, bright and expectant, as if we had mistaken the day, and the show was still to come off.

" Well, I'll be damned," said David, who was still here with some of the others, helping to clean up after the day before. " Now which of them do you suppose it was ? "

"How could it have been any of them?" I asked. "They were all here — even Pearline."

"They had plenty of friends and relatives who were not. That flag figured in a big parade of the Eastern Star or the Queens of Sheba on yesterday as ever was. Don't forget it was Sunday."

"But if they wanted it bad enough to steal it, why didn't they keep it?"

"Parade was over. Besides, it wasn't stealing; just borrowing. The same thing happened once with our crosscut saw, only that was a week-day formation. It came home on Sunday."

"It's exactly like living among monkeys," I said bitterly, remembering a few things in my own past, "and there is just as little you can do about it. Even if you catch them you never know whether you have caught the right one, and anyhow, as Kipling says, 'it isn't the shame and it isn't the blame' that you care about; it's the inconvenience — and your helplessness — and being always in the dark. . . ."

The vein was a familiar one to David. "It's coming to know that you never will know . . ." he chanted the rest of my quotation soothingly. "But this time somebody is going to find out."

But somebody never has.

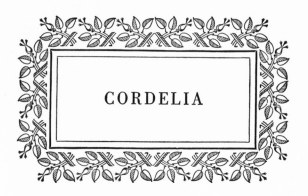

CORDELIA

IT WAS WHILE Cordelia was cooking for us that Mrs. Eldridge brought the Hindu gentleman out to tea.

Mrs. Eldridge, who lives in Memphis, lived once in the Vale of Cashmere, and surely few things could be said about a woman to equal the suggestive magic of this simple geographical statement, so redolent of bulbuls and of roses.

It has been a good many years since she left the Province of the Sun, but her friends out there do not forget her, and whenever anybody from that curve of the universe arrives in Memphis — which is oftener than one might think, owing to cotton — Mrs. Eldridge is notified and her hospitality enlisted, and on one occasion she enlisted ours to help her out with a mild and dreamy Oriental who was over here doing something of an entirely practical nature for his government. She asked if she could bring him out to tea, and I told her we would be delighted — and quite forgot to tell the servants anything about his complexion.

The first one to see him was Cordelia, as she was bringing in the tea, and since he was seated by the table with his manly trousers concealed beneath it and his turbaned head turned attentively to what I was saying, she naturally thought the visitor was both colored and a lady. Being always scrupulously careful about " ladies first," she handed him the biscuits first. I knew this was odd, coming from Cordelia, but when I saw her snatch the plate away again just as he was in the act of accepting a biscuit, and take it all the way around the table and offer it to Mrs. Eldridge, I knew that was odder. I didn't realize she was doing it because she had just seen the trousers, and I was for a moment actually panic-stricken for fear my cook was drawing some kind of color-line (in whose favor I could not make out) right there before my eyes. It was a tremendous relief when she came back with the biscuits, as soon as all the ladies had had theirs.

I don't know what she said when she returned to the kitchen, but it was not long before I saw Pearline's eye gleaming at a cautiously opened crack in the pantry door, to be replaced in time by the eye of Joe. They just simply had to see for themselves who that was in there having tea with " Miss Annie 'n' them."

I explained to them later — or tried to — that complexion wasn't everything, and Pearline bore me out.

" I had already done tol' Cordelia that he must be an Englishman or somethin'," she said.

Cordelia was for years our favorite cook. She was small and black and brainy. My mother had trained her, and over quite a long period, as reckoned by cooks, we considered her as ours even though she was by no means always there. We frequently had to make out with substitutes for months at a time while Cordelia adventured into life — in the modern sense, as opposed to cooking. But we always welcomed her back after her fling, whether with matrimony or motor cars (bought on an easy-payment plan that invariably left her cooking for the credit company instead of for us), and even once with murder. More joyfully than ever that time because it had seemed so likely that she would never be cooking for anybody any more.

It was almost too good to be true to hear her singing in the kitchen again, that first evening after her return, and I was sure the hot rolls and fried chicken were better than any even she had ever done before. I went out when she was washing the dishes to tell her so.

"We certainly are glad to have you back, Cordelia," I said, after the compliments had been duly administered, "and I think we ought to be mighty thankful, since you really did shoot Jake, that things have turned out as they have."

"Yes'm, I sho' am," Cordelia said.

"You ought to be grateful to Mr. Brewer too," I preached on, "because if he hadn't been such a good lawyer and hadn't known just what to say to the jury —"

"Oh yes, ma'm, he had done fixed the jury," said Cordelia, rather missing my meaning, but having one of her own.

It had been a close call, they said, but I do not believe she had ever entertained even the most fleeting vision of herself with a rope around her neck. She had always been the most light-hearted and sweet-tempered of human beings, and such she continued to be. I often wondered what Jake could possibly have done to so "aggravate" her, and when I would see her light her candle-end and start up the back stairs to her remote and solitary bedchamber, I used to speculate a little on the possibility of his reappearance in a form less simple to cope with than mere flesh and bone; but I honestly believe he left Cordelia's slumbers after her long day's work as untroubled as they deserved to be.

I am continually being led to modify those strong views of conscience with which I started out in life. It doesn't seem to make cowards of us any longer, or even make us uncomfortable long.

"What must Hitler's nights be like!" one of my friends exclaimed the other day at breakfast, looking up from the morning paper.

"Nice, I am sure. He sleeps just fine. Do you?" I could not resist saying, for I knew she didn't; not on account of her conscience, but because of the play she was writing. And it is possible that Hitler, himself no mean dramaturge, may also find the hours of darkness more propitious for working out his most telling scenes; but that he lies awake regretting things, I for one do not believe.

Remorse as practiced formerly, by Lady Macbeth for instance, or Eugene Aram, is rapidly losing its hold on the imagination; which must be upsetting to the moralists and the historians, and most of all, I should think, to the novelists. It was a great help to all of them, and I must confess, having formed my taste in their tradition, it was a great help to me. A malefactor untormented by a sense of guilt will always be to me a very insipid character. I should like to go backward instead of forward (for my reading, that is) in the conception of wrong-doing and its attendant discomforts — back as far as Orestes, let us say, though even this dark story is not safe from the higher criticism. Only a little while ago I was told of a college girl who was " taking " Greek Drama and who reported Agamemnon's unhappy children as saying one to the other: " If you don't kill Mother, I will " — which rather shuts the door in the face of the Furies.

But much as I hate to see them banished from literature, I have to admit that there is not room for them in a busy life. They would have been sadly in the way in the kitchen where Cordelia continued to work serenely, unmindful of the past. Sometimes as I watched the rolls and the cakes rising white and beautiful under her little black hands, I would try to picture them holding that dreadful gun; but I never could, and I don't believe anybody else could either. I would hear her on Sunday afternoons entertaining her beaux in the laundry; I would even do a little eavesdropping occasionally, because I liked to listen, and wish I might again, to her low contralto laughter as she read the " funny paper " aloud to them — " I'se got a little learnin'," she would say with modest pride — until I finally saw her marry one of them and move to town to live happy ever after on what she called (he was a World War veteran) his " bondage " from the government. And the moral is that maybe after all neither remorse nor punishment, nor even forgiveness, is as good for sin as just plain forgetting.

# THE SERVANT
# IN THE HOUSE

VISITORS in the South are seldom in anybody's house very long — a matter of minutes rather than hours I should say — without being told some story, presumably funny and generally in dialect, about what one or the other of the colored servants has been doing. Our tireless repetition of these bits of folklore is a feature of Southern culture that might well seem odd to guests from regions where what the cook said or the houseboy did has supposedly less topical significance, and I often wonder what they think of it. I have even wondered occasionally what the servants think, for the stories, whether they are funny or not, usually follow so closely on their retreating backs that they must be pretty generally overheard. I was much amused not long ago by a brief exchange that took place between the butler and the cook at a local dinner party.

"What's Miss Jennie an' them talkin' about in there?" the cook inquired as the butler came from the dining-room into the pantry and the door swung to on a burst of merriment.

"Us," was the succinct reply.

Just how this laconic gem ever got into circulation among the white folks has never been explained to me. Some day I must try to get a little more light on that point. In the meanwhile I do not vouch for the story; I merely believe it. It must have happened somewhere; it might have happened anywhere.

It would be difficult at this late day to figure out just when, or why, we ever fell into the habit of quoting and editing the conversation of our servants, but it now seems to be generally understood among us that almost any remark prefaced by " as old Uncle John said to me the other day," or " as my cook says," is to be accepted as a joke whether it ever turns into one or not. Perhaps we feel that there is something so essentially funny in the vast difference between us that little else is needed to provoke a smile, as long as one can smile.

We have been smiling a good many years now, during which the difference has not grown less, and when I think of the casual and carefree manner in which almost any one of us will take almost any one of them into the close intimacy of domestic service, without references for the most part and sometimes even sight unseen, it seems remarkable that the result should be amusing so much oftener than it is anything else. Continually do we deliver our dearest possessions, our homes and our children, into the hands of beings as unlike ourselves as is possible within the limits of a common humanity, and continually get them back again, seldom worse, often better, and invariably cleaner than they were before. Such an arrangement may reflect credit on human nature, but hardly on human intelligence; and yet, since we admit that we cannot understand the Negroes and might as well admit that we cannot get along without them, we may have hit upon the only system that will work.

I believe I have never been so romantic as Southern people often are about their colored servants. Even those of them who have served me best have habitually exasperated me in one way or another until I have wondered whether service at such a price was not too dearly bought. When I see lovely people like Will Percy and my cousin Roberta emerge from long experience similar to mine with all their sympathies still shining, it gives me such a feeling of inferiority that I am apt to be disagreeable about it. The last time I heard Roberta say: " You know I really love my servants," I was impelled to answer: " Do you? Well, I really loathe mine." That shocked her of course, just as I hoped it would, even if she didn't believe it — just as I hoped she wouldn't. For, after all, the bond between us and our Negroes is an old one and tolerable as old things become, besides being, as I once heard a man claim for baling-wire, about the only thing that holds the South together.

When I listen to slow Southern music about the black arms that are the first to hold us and the last to let us go, I know I am hearing what is not only profoundly sentimental but profoundly true. Yet I still have to give a thought to the years that lie between life's beginning and its end and remember, even as I wipe away my Southern tears, how the black arms muddle and mismanage for us through them all. And if anybody would like to know why we cannot learn to manage for ourselves — I wish I knew the answer.

It is this question that baffles me whenever I try to formulate theories about our relation to the Negroes — I really mean their relation to us, since it is they who have measured off our distance and who see that we keep it; with perfect consideration for our feelings, no doubt, but with a firmness of which we would be incapable. There are so many times when we would, for our own convenience if for no better reason, be glad to have a suspension of diplomacy and get down to something cruder, something even as raw as a fact. Everything we try to do for the colored brother — or against him, for that matter — is rendered exceedingly difficult and its results exceedingly dim by too little understanding on our part, and too much on his. In what school are they instructed, and so young, never to lower their guard — to keep always the immense advantage of inscrutability? And on the other hand why are our ways, even without instruction, so open to them?

I am convinced that we shall never know how they live among themselves, but we do know where, and we know that a one- or even a two-room cabin when it holds a growing family must hold it pretty close to nature, with small chance for the concealment or disguise of any of those matters of which nature approves. One would say that the *mores* of such an existence must be nearer animal than human, with the added disadvantage of a human vocabulary for the naming of all the unnamable things; yet our domestic servants, coming from that life into ours, never have the slightest difficulty with our imposed proprieties. I have yet to see or hear from one of them anything uncouth or unmannerly — except perhaps on the occasion of an outdoor encounter where the exigencies of snuff or tobacco may for the moment outweigh the amenities and make a little distance, or even a little dodging, advisable.

Certainly when it comes to our verbal interchanges we run a much graver risk of shocking than of being shocked. I can still remember the look of sorrow and surprise on the face of my mother's laundress when, one day in my thoughtless youth, I dashed into the kitchen calling for somebody to run and get the bull out of the garden before he ate the lilacs. Celie couldn't even raise her eyes from the shirt she was ironing as she reproved me: " Miss Annie, I ain't never heard no young lady say 'bull' in my life befo'; I don't know as I ever heard no married lady say it." And I dare say it was long, if ever, before she heard me say it again, though even then I probably knew quite as well as she did how shallow were the roots of this delicacy.

I sometimes wonder just what we think we are proving when we assert, in conformity with our facetious custom, that the only thing anybody can really know about darkies is that he can't know anything. I am sure we prefer to think of ourselves as perpetually deceived rather than perpetually distrusted, and yet the two must go together somehow.

Even the most traditional Southerner, if he stops to think about it, must realize that in nothing that touches them deeply do even the friendliest of his colored friends like to have him share. They will invite him to their weddings and their funerals and make him welcome, as the saying is, if he appears, but he must hear, if he has ears, the rising tempo in their laughter or their lamentation as he departs, and so measure the restraint caused by his presence. I have always felt sure I was not wanted either in their grief or in their joy and I only wish they didn't want me when they are in jail, for it embarrasses me beyond measure to see them there and to try to talk to them as if they weren't, with those ridiculous iron bars between me and their familiar faces.

Negroes, no matter what they have done, always seem to me completely out of place in the hands of the law. Besides, with the ones I have known, there was always so much for them to do at home; Aunt Althea, for instance, who was the best nurse I ever saw; and Cordelia, who was almost the best cook.

We have never learned the truth about Aunt Althea. There was a mystery there which the years have done nothing to dispel. But I shall never forget how wretched

we all were through the miserable ordeal of her arrest
and the things that followed it — all of us except Aunt
Althea, who was upheld by either her perfect innocence
or her perfect guilt, while we could only writhe in our
uncertainty.

It was the summer Betty came to visit us with her
baby, and we had considered ourselves supremely fortunate to be able to get Aunt Althea for a nurse, for she
made her living not by going out to work but by running a sort of miniature orphanage at home. She had
lived for years in a two-room cabin with a " dog run "
between, set back under a persimmon tree in the corner
of Mr. Weakley's field, not far from our back pasture.
There was a sketchy paling fence enclosing a yard not
much bigger than a play-pen around the cabin, where
her small black boarders rolled and tumbled in the dust,
except when it was raining. Then she must have managed somehow to tumble them all inside. Rain or shine,
the fence was always festooned with their funny little
clothes, all washed and patched; and Aunt Althea herself was always as neat as a pin in her bright cotton
dresses and her white " head pieces."

Nobody ever inquired where the " orphans " came
from; it was too easy to guess; but everybody said she
was unbelievably good to them. They grew up a bit of
course as time went by, and were passed on to their

various destinies, but that only left room for more just like them. It never occurred to anyone to look for changes in that corner of Mr. Weakley's field.

And then one windy morning in March the cabin was not there any more, and nothing to mark the spot where it had stood but a little heap of ashes — unbelievably little — and the bricks of the fallen chimney and the cistern top. But the orphans were all safe. Aunt Althea had them well out in the field among the cotton stalks, wrapped in quilts, and croker-sacks, before the first help arrived. She was quiet and efficient through the whole business and rather took advantage of the prevailing excitement to find homes for her " chil'en " among the friends and neighbors who had gathered to watch the blaze. To find a home for herself would have been all too easy; her reputation as a nurse had been high in the community before she ever embarked on the orphanage. She had even had " hospital experience " as a young woman, so they said. But she wanted to " res' herself " and visit her relatives in Arkansas, and she availed herself of this act of God to do it. Her return to the neighborhood and Betty's visit coincided, and that was how I managed to get her to nurse the baby.

" I just don't know what I am going to do when I have to take Elizabeth away from her," Betty declared over and over again as the long hot days went by. " You

don't suppose there is any chance of inducing her to
go east with us. . . ."

I did not suppose so, and one day I broke it to my
guest that we might not even be able to keep Aunt
Althea till the end of her visit, for Mr. Weakley had
started building a new cabin in his field where the old
one used to be, and I was sure she was planning to move
into it. I had noticed her going up there with the baby
when the men were working, and she already referred
to it as " my house." " She is probably up there right
now," I said, " hot as it is. You must tell her to keep
your daughter out of the sun. I am really surprised at
her."

But they came in as I was speaking, fresh and cool
from the hammock under the pecan tree. I have not
forgotten any of the things that happened that afternoon. I remember how Aunt Althea put the baby down
on the matting at our feet and announced that she was
goin' to make us all some lemonade. " It sho' is hot," she
said, moving off in the direction of the kitchen.

She came back in a very few minutes without the
lemonade, more upset than I had ever seen her. She had
evidently heard something in the kitchen to excite her.
" What's Mr. Weakley an' them goin' to do to my ole
cistern?" she asked in a voice that was not her own.

" What do you mean?" I said. " Doesn't it have to be

cleaned out and repaired before anybody can use it?"

"That cistern don't need nothin' done to it cep'n to mend it roun' the top where the bricks done got broke," she said, and I was sure I saw her arm trembling as she stooped down to gather up the baby; "I'se g'wine up there to see about it right now."

"No, Aunt Althea," Betty said; "it's too hot. Take Elizabeth back to the swing. Besides, I don't want her around where they are cleaning out cisterns and things; it's not sanitary."

Aunt Althea went out in the direction indicated, but I felt the change that had come over her. The sense of the unknown was rising about me like a miasma. "Watch her," something seemed to whisper; and so I watched.

She went back to the pecan tree, put the baby in the hammock, and began pulling gently on the rope, but I noticed that she did not sit down beside it in her comfortable chair. She stood there swinging the hammock back and forth in silence for a while and then began to sing:

> "This worl' is not my home, Lo'd Jesus,
> Lo'd Jesus, lif' my soul. . . ."

Her voice rose higher and higher and the hammock began gaining in speed, until suddenly, with one quick glance over her shoulder toward the house, she took up the baby and started walking, as casually as her evident haste permitted, toward the garden.

The gate was open, but she did not go in; instead, she passed on around the wall and so out of my view — until I could get to one of the upstairs windows and look out over the roof. Down by the pond she went and across the pasture, toward Mr. Weakley's field. She was running now, still holding the baby easily in her accustomed arms, and she must have run all the way except when she had to stoop under the barbed-wire fences, but when she got there it was too late. They had found the small bundle wrapped up in a piece of blanket; they had already dragged it up from the mud of the old cistern where it had lain weighted down with a flat-iron. . . .

I am not often in sympathy with what is called concerted feeling. Human beings are not at their best when they are functioning as a mob, and even as a community they never seem to be quite as clear about what they are doing as even excited people often are when they are acting by themselves. I do not like to remember, and I shall certainly not try to relate, some of the things that were said and done — or at least begun — in our "aroused neighborhood," as the newspapers called it,

during the twenty-four hours or so that followed Aunt
Althea's arrest. Everybody was outraged, without knowing either then or later what they were outraged about.
The only person who knew that was Aunt Althea and
she just wouldn't tell. She stood before her accusers as
silent as a stone and let the storm break over her. They
flung words at her which she did not understand and
others that she did — such as " murder " and " white "
— but got none in reply. Though I do not know to this
good day whether by her silence she was protecting herself or guarding some secret entrusted to her, I have
never doubted her wisdom in acting as she did. There
were no witnesses against her, and all her past among
us — the known part of it — was eloquent in her praise.
In the end there was no lynching and really very little
" law." It just seemed better all round to buy her a one-
way ticket and let her go for an indefinite sojourn with
her relatives in Arkansas.

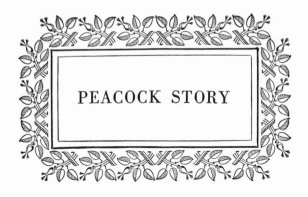

PEACOCK STORY

It was the summer Harriet was here from Vassar visiting Mary that we lost the peacock.

Nobody could ever imagine how he happened to wander away, unless one of the other peacocks was fighting him and making his home so unhappy that he decided to go in search of a new one. We spent our days looking for him, scouring the country in all directions, and Harriet confided to me that she got up in the night every time she heard a noise in the yard and went out on her balcony to see if it could be the wanderer coming home. She was so sweet and sympathetic about my anxiety that I wouldn't for the world have laughed at the idea of a fowl of any description getting down from its perch and roaming about in the night.

We had put an advertisement in the paper the first thing, under the "Lost, Strayed, or Stolen" caption: "One peacock. — Handsome reward." Only they had got the punctuation wrong and printed it: "One peacock — Handsome. — Reward." He had never had a name before, but he had one now of course — and an understatement at that, for all the glory of his summer plumes.

It almost broke my heart to think of him trailing that splendor through underbrush and blackberry thickets, but it was even worse when I imagined him emerging on the open road to be chased by boys and run down by automobiles.

I do not know how many days and nights I spent entertaining these unhappy visions before all at once we began to hear, through Joe and Lucy and the others, rumors of his appearance in various localities — all of them miles apart, and miles away from us.

"Jesse Brown say he seed him Sunday; he come up out of the gulley back of his house. He say he didn' know what kind of a bird he was; he ain't never seed no peacock befo'."

[ 169 ]

"But why didn't he catch him? Which way did he go?" I would ask in anguish. But Jesse did not know; nor Mr. Harris, who had seen him down in the bottom when he was going fishing; nor old Aunt Molly, though he had come right up an' et with her chickens twicet las' week.

Then one day we got a clue that we could follow. Back in a cotton field, a mile or more from the road, lived Ophelian and Caledonia his wife, whom we knew well — too well; and as soon as word was brought to me that my peacock had been seen in that vicinity, my hopes rose with a bound. If anybody could "catch up" Handsome for me it was surely Ophelian, else had his years been spent in vain.

We jumped into the car and hurried there — or as near there as the furrows permitted — and then got out and fairly ran the rest of the way, for it had occurred to us as we came along that the catching-up might already have taken place and had a fatal ending.

But no. Caledonia was blithe and reassuring. "Lawd, Miss Annie, didn' nobody tell me he was yourn. Yes'm, he sho' do come up every night an' roos' in that there walnut tree. Ophelian say he mus' be a new kind of turkey or sump'n."

She was sure that Ophelian with her assistance could

[ 170 ]

catch him that very night, and we agreed to be on hand as soon as it was dark, to bestow the reward and take the truant home.

The girls thought it was a great lark — almost as good as a possum-hunt — but I felt very tense as we bumped over the furrows again that evening and saw the cabin and the walnut tree silhouetted against the rising moon. I had worked myself into an almost superstitious state of mind over my silly peacock and couldn't really believe I was destined ever to lay eyes on him again.

But there he was, hunched up on one of the high limbs, and looking indeed, with all his lacy feathers gone, much more like a turkey than a peacock — more like a bedraggled buzzard than either one.

Caledonia and Ophelian were lurking in the shadows, with several of their neighbors who had come to lend a hand and enjoy the sport. They were suppressed and silent and as stealthy as cats, every one of them. Nobody responded to our whispered greeting; they just moved in a little nearer to the tree.

Then suddenly, without sound or signal, one of the men stepped forward under the lowest of the overhanging limbs and stooped over, bracing his hands on the muscles above his knees. With one astonishing movement Ophelian leapt upon his shoulders and grasped the limb, then swung himself lightly up. The peacock stirred and settled down again.

I felt my heart actually pounding as I watched that still ascent — that creeping silence, dark against the moon. The peacock put out his head, then drew it back. Ophelian was close enough now to grab his legs. Would the motionless arm that was yet somehow moving never dart forward and clutch and hold? . . .

It did. Everything, that is, except hold. Ophelian's technique was faultless, but he had been trained in a lighter school, and Handsome, even after a month of locusts and wild honey, was too heavy for the one-handed hook-off. I didn't quite see what happened. I heard the girls, who had been holding their breath, let it out again in a simultaneous squeal which was lost in the devastating scream a peacock makes when he thinks he has won. Spreading his denuded wings, poor Handsome swooped as best he could to earth and started to run for it, but Caledonia and the others were upon him so swiftly that I heard my agonized " Oh, catch him! " ring out well after he was already caught.

That final onslaught just about finished his feathers, but his legs, as we tied them ignominiously together with a strip from Caledonia's " piece of apron," were to all appearances as good as ever, and Ophelian bore him off in triumph to the car.

There had been an indefiniteness about the term "handsome reward" which was altogether intentional. We had meant all the time to go a little beyond the reasonable expectations of whoever might be the one to claim it — rich man, poor man, beggar man, thief. . . . Ophelian, who came easily within three of these categories, was sufficiently dazzled by the two dollar bills I put into his hand after he deposited my bird on the floor of the automobile.

"And tell Caledonia I have a dress for her," I called back as we bounded away across the moonlit billows of the cotton field, remembering a Paris model from which Paris had long since departed, in a lovely shade of green that would delight Caledonia's soul and be very trying to her complexion.

In the weeks that followed, I spent a lot of time trying to guard my diminished fowl from insult and injury, both to his person and to his pride. I knew only too well what the other peacocks would do to him if they got a chance, and I was even afraid of what he might do to himself if he caught sight of his changed reflection in the glass of the long windows where he liked to stand. Probably fly at it in a fury of repudiation, I thought. And it seemed to me his new feathers were incredibly slow in growing.

Then one morning, just as he was beginning to register improvement, we woke to find him gone again. Joe brought in the news as we were sitting down to breakfast — " An' this time sump'n done cotch him sho' nuf. I done foun' the place, jus' this side the bob-wire fence down by the spring-house. His feathers is all roun' on the groun'."

One glance at the terrain was enough to substantiate Joe's theory; but what " varmint " was large enough to make way with so large a bird? Not a possum surely, and it was long since we had had a fox anywhere around, or a law-breaking dog. Mary and Joe and I went down on our knees simultaneously to look for silvan footprints on the ground, but Harriet, who had no preconceptions as to the probable nature of our beasts of prey, stood up and looked around her, and presently she pounced upon a place where the fence wire was sagging between two posts.

" What would you call that? " she demanded, untwisting from one of the barbs something that looked like a small green feather, but wasn't.

" I knew it was silk the minute I saw it," Harriet said excitedly. " It looks as if it came off of that dress you gave Caledonia."

" Good old Harrie! " Mary exclaimed, with a glance at me and then one at Joe, who was fortunately out of earshot at the moment. It was as plain as day, of course;

there could no longer be any doubt as to the nature of the varmints. They had not stolen him the first time; that had merely given them the idea; that was just good luck. But it was going to be good management from now on, and I would be redeeming peacocks for the rest of my days. . . .

Whose move was it now? the girls wanted to know.

It was ours of course. We didn't breathe a word of our discovery to the servants, but I told them somebody must see Caledonia or her husband right away and tell them the peacock was lost again. It was barely possible, I said without a quiver, that the poor bird might have got away from whatever caught him and would be going back to roost in the walnut tree.

"I seed Caledonia at church Sunday," Pearline, who was ironing, informed me. "She done 'bout wore out that dress you give her. She ain't had it off her back. Yes'm; I'll tell her."

After that there was nothing to do but wait, so we waited. I was confident that one of them would come to see me as soon as they got the message, and sure enough, on the very next day we saw Caledonia coming across the pasture from the "big road," the flounces of her Paris gown dangling about her knees. We watched her unhurried progress through the back yard and heard her easy greeting to the occupants of the kitchen.

" Send her on in," I called to Lucy; " I'll talk to her in here."

In she came, with breezy assurance, fanning herself lightly with her hat.

" Sit down, Caledonia." I indicated the window-seat, where the sun came in and lit the remaining luster of the green silk dress. I saw Harriet eyeing it with an answering gleam — that of the successful sleuth.

" Miss Pearline sont word your peacock done gone again. He sho' don't like to stay home, do he? "

" Has either of you seen him this time? " I inquired.

" No'm. I sho' ain't, nor 'Phelian neither."

" Well, I just wanted to tell you both to keep a good lookout and let me know immediately when — if — you do. Don't wait to come; go somewhere and telephone."

I knew they would feel obliged to let a decent interval elapse before they " found " him, but it was no more than that. We had put in less than twenty-four hours of listening for the telephone and jumping every time it rang before the expected tidings came over the wire. Caledonia's light insouciant voice informed us that everything had happened just as I had hoped it would; they had already caught the peacock and put him in the house. And there a half-hour later we found him, aimlessly pecking about on the floor of their bedroom.

I broke it to them at some length that all rewards, both present and future, were out of the question, and they were visibly disappointed, as was only natural, but not in the least embarrassed, which was something more.

"Lawd, Miss Annie," Caledonia said, " you knows I wouldn't do nothin' like that, nor 'Phelian neither. We'd ruther ast you for the money if we was in sich a tight; but we ain't never in no tight. They pays 'Phelian two dollars an' six bits ev'y day he works over at the Buckeye. Mr. Perkins done sont over yistiddy to ast him when's he comin' back."

Caledonia did all the talking. Ophelian at least maintained the grace of silence and neither denied my accusations nor made any comment on the evidence I advanced in support of them.

"Yes'm, it sho' do look like a piece of my dress," his wife conceded glibly as I laid Harriet's shred of green silk against the matching garment she still wore. " I 'bout hung up in the bob-wire goin' th'ough that way to see my sister; the one what lives over there on Mr. Murray's place."

What hope was there, what hope is there ever, of proving anything, with sisters and alibis in every direction? Of course we can hale them before the magistrate and before the judge, and sometimes we do, but not

often. " Agree with thine adversary quickly " seems to
work best, even when it works backwards; so we agreed
— I not to reward them for stealing my peacock, and
they not to steal him again.

But I did counsel Ophelian, before we drove away,
to report for work at the Buckeye Mill the very next
morning, and told him I intended to call up Mr. Perkins and find out if he had done so.

I spoke as severely as possible, leaning out of the car,
where he had again deposited the peacock, in order to
sound final and forceful; but I was already beginning
to feel unpleasantly sorry instead of just pleasantly mad.
He looked so innocent and respectful standing there
among the cotton stalks waiting for me to finish that
I didn't say nearly as much as I intended to before we
bumped away.

# THE
# MAGNOLIA TREE

Not HALF enough has been said and done about magnolias, though a good many people have tried to give them their due in prose and rhyme and a good many others have done what they could to " immortalize " them on canvas. But still that part of the human race that lives where magnolias do not grow has to be continually excused for not knowing the difference between the native magnolia of the South, which is a forest tree, immense in size, holding immense white blossoms to the sky, and the exotic little trees we plant in gardens everywhere. The spring tourist continues to make his annual remark among us: " Why, haven't the magnolias begun to bloom yet down here? Ours have . . ." and I continue to think he ought to know better. I should like to lead him up to a small brass plate that says: *Magnolia grandiflora. Habitat,* etc. . . . Only I wouldn't want it to be on one of my trees. One of the things I like best about them is that they belong here so much more radically than I do that the name plate ought really to be on me.

I think the beauty of growing things should seem greater to us when we live with them than when we make them live with us, though this is not the accepted view. Most gardeners would miss the sense of triumph they get from cajoling something to live where it would rather not be. I believe too they like to feel that it could not get along without them — a sort of canary-bird or goldfish complex. Perhaps it is because I am not a good gardener that I feel the other way. I like vegetation to be pruned and trimmed, but at the same time I like to know that with me out of the way it could, as someone has very charmingly said, spring back to the thicket like a deer.

If I didn't feel about the magnolias that they will be here blooming away for ages after I am somewhere else

— picking silly asphodels maybe — I certainly wouldn't break off great branches of them the way I do, to bring into the house. Even as it is, I am often impelled to stay my hand, there is something so untouchable about their special kind of loveliness. They are so chiseled and so still they lay a hush upon the heart.

But they are really quite as beautiful indoors, standing about in big bowls and jars, and now that it has become permissible and " æsthetic " to go on admiring them even after they have turned brown, we can have less regret that their whiteness is so brief. In contrast to most flowers, they are aromatic to the end, and when I empty out the water and see it so clear and their dark stems so clean, I am reminded of things I have read about saintly people lying unaltered in their coffins.

I am more sentimental over magnolias than I approve of being, but they would forgive me if they knew how small I was when I began to feel that way about them. I believe most little children are touched by the sharp contrast between the dark tree and the white blossoms. They always like to stand by the trunk and look up through the branches. Grown people should try it too sometimes, to learn the real meaning of the word " crepuscular." Strange things used to be revealed to my imagination in that strange twilight, and I suppose that is why I never seem to have experienced the least difficulty in believing it was under the tallest and the blackest of the magnolias on our lawn that Mrs. Latham lost her leg.

" It was right on that spot whar you'se standin' at," my nurse had said to me, and I seem to have thought over a period of years that the loss had occurred in the same way that Mrs. Latham might have lost her umbrella or her fan. I do not know just when I began to realize it had not been anywhere near as easy as that, but the slow and painful result of a gunshot wound inflicted by her young son, who was shooting at a snake.

It was already an old story before it was ever told to me at all, for it had happened back in the " yellow-fever days " when people came to stay with their friends in the country under the impression that there their perils would be less. Mrs. Latham, having contracted a bullet in the knee instead of yellow fever, would doubtless have been much better off in town, where she could have had a doctor without a delay of twenty-four mortal hours. It still makes me unhappy to think of her sufferings, but I have sometimes turned to them as a sort of antidote when I found myself being too unhappy about her son, for, after all, Mrs. Latham was only a victim, whereas John was a martyr.

They were bound together and set apart by a sense of tragedy that was not allowed to lapse for a moment.

John never seemed to take his eyes off his mother. He read her wishes by a sort of clairvoyance and leapt to anticipate her every movement; and if move she must, he leapt again to offer his young shoulder to her arm. I believe she had a wooden leg, of the less expert manufacture those days afforded, but dresses were full and long and one could not be quite sure. The crutch, however, was visible enough, and so was John, and between the two she made out rather well. She had a big downstairs bedroom when she was at home, and most of her life was spent in hotels where there were elevators.

She was a beautiful woman, which somehow made it worse for John. Everybody in speaking of her misfortune always ended on that note, as if it deprived the accident of its last shred of excuse — " Such a beautiful woman, too! " — but it really had been unavoidable on John's part. His mother had told him to shoot the snake, and then cried: " Don't shoot it," and jumped forward to scare it away just as John was pulling the trigger. Being unable to shoot and not shoot at the same time was John's only fault in the matter, but it had altered his life completely.

His career of sacrifice began so early that he seemed to find it quite easy by the time he was a young man to give up practically all the things other young men wanted — or just not to want them, as being easier still.

But when it came to giving up Martha, it was not easy. Then he really needed help, and Martha refused to give him any. Instead she made it harder for him by her complete lack of sympathy with his point of view.

"Your mother likes me, you know," she said, "and it would not hurt her a bit to have to lean on my arm some of the time, while yours took a little rest." That was, he knew, her light and figurative way of suggesting an unthinkable change in his mother's attitude, and in his own.

But Martha did not find it unthinkable. In fact, she gave two whole summers to thinking about it; one in England, where John and his mother had taken a " very convenient " cottage, and another in Brittany, where they knew a " most comfortable " hotel. After that she gave it up and spent her summers less conveniently and comfortably, marrying at the close of one of them a man whom she had met in Switzerland on some Alp or other that the young ladies of that period were permitted to climb.

He was an Englishman in the diplomatic service and going up in other ways than mountains, and Martha soon developed what she always spoke of as a very full life, though she continued to find time to spill over occasional letters into John's empty one. He would hand them to my mother to read, watching her face as she did so, to be sure she was not missing any of Martha's sweetness or her wit. They all began: " My very dear John," and ended: " Ever yours " — whatever that might mean. Then he would fold them up and put them methodically back in his black morocco pocketbook. He had turned into an old bachelor overnight, my mother used to say, and the added freedom he enjoyed as time went on and Mrs. Latham grew heavier and more stationary was really not an enjoyment at all, because he didn't know what to do with it.

These were the years when we saw him most frequently. Many people used to feel that to be near my mother was for some reason to be nearer to their heart's desire, and John was one of those who would take the long trek out on the street-car and the long walk at the end of it, even in the coldest winter weather, for the sake of those warm hours by the fire when he could talk or even think about Martha with somebody who plainly understood everything.

" I'm afraid you found it terribly cold dressing in your room without a fire," my mother said to him one exceedingly frosty morning when he appeared for breakfast, literally blue with cold.

" Oh, not at all," he assured her, maintaining a polite distance from the blazing logs in the dining-room fireplace that were drawing the rest of us like a magnet;

"I experienced some slight difficulty in fastening my collar button, but after I lighted the lamp and warmed my fingers over the chimney for a moment, I managed very nicely."

I am apt to remember this when I hear about the courtesy of other days — or the heroism, for that matter.

It was quite a surprise to everybody when Mrs. Latham, after staying within the radius of American resorts for a good many years, decided one summer to go abroad again. John was perhaps as much surprised as anybody, and more pleased than he had seemed to be about anything for a long time. It would mean being at least one ocean nearer to Martha. She was in Venice, he told my mother, where Violet was studying art; Sir Richard was still in India. It was hard to realize that Martha could have a daughter almost grown, he said, just as he always did whenever he spoke of Violet.

They did not return at the end of the summer. Mrs. Latham, it seemed, was very contented in her old haunts and was making no plans about coming home. Of himself John wrote little; and of Martha not at all. My mother supposed this was because he had not seen her, or maybe because he had found her greatly changed; but in the end, when he finally did come back and told her his strange story, she knew that both these suppositions had been wrong. For he had seen Martha that first summer, and thought her lovelier than ever, but could not bear to write about either their meeting or their parting, because by that time she was dead. . . . "And I was the only one who knew it, and I had to go and leave her lying there alone. . . ." He kept his pleasant voice on an even key, but my mother noticed how hard and white the knuckles stood out on the thin old-bachelor hands he held together on his knee.

Martha knew she had that kind of heart, but she didn't want anybody else to know it; Sir Richard had to be in India for another year, and Violet was at the age where a mother was a great convenience in her life. "But she wanted me to know," John said; "I believe she wanted me to know everything; and we had three whole days together, and that was, for me, a great deal."

Three days out of all those years. . . . It seemed too frail a benefit to support the immense weight of gratitude he kept heaping upon it as he described the hours, one by one, that he had spent alone with Martha in the tiny mountain hotel — or rather out of it, for the weather had been beautiful. There had even been a moon. . . .

It was perhaps because Martha had known about her heart that she had written to him to join her there. Violet was with Sir Richard's sister in Switzerland, and Martha wrote she might never again be as free as she found herself in this quiet little place — certainly not as free and as near to heaven at the same time, and she went on to tell him about the view from her window.

Even in John's mind, where the lode-star of his own desire generally rose so clouded with doubts that he did not try to follow it, there was not any doubt about the rectitude of his course on this occasion. His mother was agreeably occupied with her cure at some Baden or other in Germany; he was even not very far from the little Austrian village where Martha's letter had been posted, and the next day he was on the train.

It used to seem strange to me that anyone in his pre-occupied state of mind should have been so impressed with the setting and the atmosphere of his great adventure. I had to do a good deal of living myself before I learned how sensitive the whole human machine becomes as we drive it into joy or into danger, but I came in time to understand quite well how every aspect of that stony valley with the little gray church looking down on it, and the little inn, whose mistress was gray and stony too, had taken on for him a high relief, so that not even Martha as he saw her there, either in life or in death, was more clearly outlined in his memory.

They could not do much walking because it was all up, from there, and bad for her heart, so they sat a great deal under the plane tree in the garden of the little inn.

Sometimes the village people would come for beer, and once there was a wedding party that had possession of the inn all day; and that was perhaps their happiest day of all, because they took their lunch and ate it by the little trout-stream. It mattered so little where they were, because they could talk forever anywhere. That was what she had missed most in her life, Martha said. Crowds of people all the time and no one to talk to. "I think sometimes that has made Richard a little jealous — of my past, I mean," she added quickly. This was almost the only time she had referred in any way to the place John had held in her life, but she had talked to him a great deal about himself, and once, after looking at him thoughtfully for a while, she had spoken about what she called his beautiful patience and wished he had been able to share it with her long ago.

"I asked her if her life had been happy," John said, flushing a little at the memory, " and she answered, just as she always wrote in her letters, that it had been full."

They had all their meals in the garden at the little table under the plane tree, but John got up so much earlier in the morning than she did that he would take a good long walk up the valley before breakfast, and then scramble down a steeper way and drop into the garden almost from the treetops, to surprise her, like a foolish boy. She would be there waiting for him — keeping the coffee weak and the rolls hard, she said — and they would have breakfast as if they meant to go on having it together for the rest of their lives. And it was the rest of hers, for on the fourth morning when John swung himself down into the garden she was not there.

He went into the kitchen in search of Fräulein Lotte, his heart already pounding so from his exercise that he tried to think sudden terror had nothing to do with it, and then, remembering that Fräulein Lotte would of course have gone to market at that hour, he ran up the little wooden stairs and knocked lightly on Martha's door. He thought he heard her say come in, but so faintly that he was more frightened than ever; yet when he opened the door and realized at once that she was not asleep, but dead, he was for some reason not frightened at all. It might have been the perfect calmness of her face as she lay there on the white pillow with the blue air of the mountains stirring the curtain of her open window, or it may have been that the happiness of the last three days had somehow warned him, but he knew that this was what they had come for — both of them — and that for her, at least, all was well.

For the first few minutes he even thought it might be well for him too, but then of course he realized it could not be — not yet at any rate. There were things he would have to do, to think about; and as soon as he began to think about them in this practical way, he saw for the first time that there might even be things he would have to explain. It came over him with a sort of shock that he and Martha were after all not old; that she at least was young and lovely, lying there, in a way he had not thought about her since she was a girl. What was she doing here alone with him? He would certainly be asked that; and to whom would he have to answer first? To Violet, who was too young to understand, or Sir Richard's sister, who, whatever her age, might still not understand? It was strange that anything so innocently plain should have such possibilities of confusion. He could no longer see his presence there as anything but an injury to Martha. There was nothing he could do for her now except not to be there at all — not only to be gone, but never to have been there. Then suddenly he saw that this miracle of reversal in time and space was one that he had it in his power to perform. Fräulein Lotte had never learned his name or mastered his identity in any way. For her he could vanish as completely by catching a train some five miles down the valley as if the earth had swallowed him, and nobody else knew he was there — not even his mother.

He packed his bag and laid the money for his bill on the table in his room. Then going back once more where Martha lay, he glanced at her desk to be sure the letters he had noticed lying there had her daughter's address on them, her sister-in-law's, her husband's; and without looking at her again, he went down the little wooden stairs and out the door. . . .

" I was right to do it," he said, perhaps in answer to some question in my mother's eyes; " I know that I was right because it was so hard. Every step I took down the valley was harder for me than if I had been climbing the steepest mountain there. . . . I wanted to go back so much. . . ."

It was late in the summer afternoon when he finished his story, sitting with my mother on the stone bench near the magnolia tree where life's code of conduct had been laid down for him. Watching the darkness deepen under the branches that had grown so wide since then, my mother wondered whether John had any picture in his mind of the boy with the gun who had entered that shadow so many years ago. She felt that he had been a great deal too hard on him through all of them.

# SUMMER

SUMMER HAS COME over the top with all its batteries in action. These first really hot days seem always the worst, and if one is foolish enough to start multiplying them by all that are to come, one's plight seems desperate indeed. Whether to faint or fly appears then the only alternative. But we who have weathered so many summers here without doing either of these things have learned some others we can do instead, and after a bit of early languishing and complaining we always manage to pull ourselves together and set about mitigating our condition in a variety of ways.

The most original of these is the system we have devised of taking down all the windows and doors on the front of the house, which faces south, and storing them away and forgetting there has ever been anything but screens between us and the outside world. A southern exposure is a wonderful thing in this latitude. All the openings where the winter sun came in are now in shadow, admitting only the breeze, which, when it blows at all in summer, is always on that side — a cosmic arrangement which fits in perfectly with ours. We are very proud of it and feel that, since nature's schemes and our own so often fail to coincide, it can hardly be praised too highly. But nobody ever dreams of praising it until he has asked us what we do when it rains. Strange to say, we do not have to do anything; I have never known just why. It may rain in at the southern windows of other houses, but it never has in ours, and it was precisely this observation that decided us to take them out. Sometimes in the course of the summer we may have to lower the Venetian blinds until an exceptionally boisterous shower blows by, but that is seldom and that is all.

It makes a delightful change in the look of things to have the windows gone, not to mention the difference in the feeling. I have always thought it was strange the way we wall ourselves in and then depend for all our avenues of joy on knocking holes in the wall — the bigger the better always.

When I came into the parlor this morning I seemed to be stepping out of doors — a modulated out-of-doors, shaded from sun, shielded from insects, and yet all there before me. The wide slats of the blinds were turned to let in a tempered light on the freshly laundered slipcovers, and much of the garden had come in with the roses and the larkspur gathered yesterday in the cool of the evening (if one can call it that), which is the only time to gather anything out there these days, except perhaps a sunstroke. I don't even go out any more to see how Joe is getting on with his weeding. I dare say I should be surprised.

It is altogether too hot for visitors, but I have one. Stephen has been here more than a month now, and has said nothing so far about going away again — ever. He is really Roberta's guest and not mine. He only came to me because she has gone east for the summer, according to her unvarying custom, guests or no guests, as soon as the hot weather strikes the Delta.

"We hate terribly to go off and make him move," she wrote to me, "just when he is getting his work so well in hand. He has done some sketches of the plantation — the darkies especially — that are as good as anything I ever saw. If we were not taking the servants with us I would just leave the house open and him in it; he doesn't seem to know it is hot. But, after all, he can keep right on painting at your house, the landscape and the figures are so much the same."

Stephen is " painting the South." It is thus he accounts for his presence among us, and he has accepted the change of hostesses without embarrassment. The role of guest suits him admirably and he fills it with grace. His own home is in England, but his childhood, which still hangs about him somehow, was spent in France, and he can be very amusing in the languages of both countries. I do not think his artistic talent is as great as many people consider it, but it never fails him, and his enthusiasm for all branches of his subject never runs dry.

" Of course I realize I have got to really study the psychology of your blacks, and your sharecroppers too, before I shall be able to paint them as I mean to do," he announced this morning, keeping his thumb in the book he had been reading since before breakfast; " and I ought to have a better understanding of their economic outlook. I have really got to master your whole agrarian system."

I couldn't help speculating a little on just what bearing such commendable thoroughness might have on an already extended hospitality, but of course I didn't mention it, and when he presently threw Herbert Agar aside and went out into the back yard, where Bertha was preparing to pick the geese, I went too and was soon almost as much excited as he was over the prospect of getting some really vivid sketches of the proceeding.

This event, which enlivens one day of every summer and turns the back premises into a sort of rodeo, has always seemed to me to have its picturesque moments, but I had not realized how greatly it would be prolonged by the artistic considerations Stephen now brought to bear on it. The lights and darks of the background, Joe's attitudes (he didn't know before that he had any and thought he was merely holding the geese), and Bertha's costume all had to be checked and changed. I had to rush upstairs and tear up an old pillow-case to make her a whiter " headpiece " and then fold it and pin it on because she was already engaged in plucking one of the victims, and change the white meal-sack she was putting the feathers into for " something with more color."

Perhaps no one could paint geese to suit me, but Bertha certainly picks them admirably; by which I mean, in the second place, that she gets a world of beautiful feathers, and in the first place that the geese do not seem to mind it particularly. What they really do mind is being caught up; that giddy operation over, they settle down on Bertha's ample lap, with Joe holding their legs, and lose interest. Being immortalized on canvas, however, turned out to be more of an ordeal than being put into pillows.

" Might I have that big fellow over again for a minute — the one with the black bill? You needn't pluck him any more if you have finished, but just catch him up and hold him a bit; I like his expression rather better. . . ."

I could only hope the supernumerary nervous vibrations caused by all this repetition were not being absorbed by the feathers billowing out the bag at Bertha's right hand. I have always indulged a sentiment about having my pillows made from live geese, but by the same token they should not, I suppose, be too lively. Contented cows; unagitated geese. . . . If we keep on we will be wanting to gauge the mental condition of all our animals before we despoil them, in somewhat the way Stephen feels about understanding the psychology of his " blacks " before he paints them.

I had to tell him, as the noon hour approached, that both the plucking and the pantomime would have to come to a close and let Bertha and the geese go free, but he begged for a few more minutes, to grab his camera and take some recording shots.

The Ciné-Kodak which he brought with him to supplement the work of brush and pencil in portraying the Southern scene, he always keeps hung somewhere about his person or within easy reach, on the arm of a chair or the limb of a tree, so determined is he not to miss any of the more fluent aspects of our land and labors. I often wonder how he can afford the miles of film devoured by that little machine, assuming always that he is as penniless as he proclaims himself to be. When and where will those countless little rolls which he numbers and stores away like so many chrysalises, take on their counterfeited life and flutter — on what walls? It gives me a nostalgic feeling to imagine these familiar glimpses being evoked again at will for unfamiliar eyes.

"Did your laundress carry buckets of water on her head when she was growing up, to give her that superb *démarche*?" he asked me the other day. "She walks like a goddess." He was loading his camera as he spoke, and since it was early on a Monday morning I surmised that he was about to level it on Cleo, Pearline's daughter, who would be coming to wash.

Cleo is tall and slim and moves with an Olympian leisure. I watched her swinging across the dewy lawn, with what I tried to make an artist's eyes, and I could see, I thought, just what he hoped to capture as he released the mechanism of his camera and followed her approach with its recording eye.

He had partially concealed himself behind a syringa

bush — he didn't want to make the nymph self-conscious, he explained — but as she came abreast of him her face was turned the other way, and I wondered how he was going to manage to make her look around without startling her. If he had simply bawled out, as Randolph or David or any one of our native sons would have done: " Hi, Cleo, look this way a minute," all would have been well; she would have looked, have seen the camera for what it was, and thrown in a grin for good measure; but instead he uttered his greeting in the softest of small voices. " Hel-lo," he cooed from his syringa bush, and Cleo leapt into the air. Never in her life, I feel sure, had she been accosted in a tone like that; certainly not by a young gentleman ambushed in the shrubbery.

I had to admit as he deplored his film that in this case a little more psychology would certainly have helped.

Today is too hot for anybody to work out in the sun, even Joe, so I have put him to cleaning up the tool-shed which is at least dark, though nobody could say cool. Stephen, who fared forth as usual after breakfast with camera and brush, but speedily returned to the shadow of the thick walls, is being so energetic within them that it exhausts me even to look on. My own exertions are confined to the minimum necessary to dissuade him from rehanging all the pictures — mine, not his. Since it is too hot for him to be painting new ones, he has fallen-to upon the old. In his case art is certainly long.

I dare say my pictures could be shifted — in some cases perhaps eliminated — to advantage, but they have been there a long time, most of them; so long, in fact, that I have practically ceased to see them, but I should certainly see the marks on the wall-paper. And besides I don't want to be made self-conscious about my pictures, as to either their artistic merit or the places where they have gradually come to hang — I might almost say hang themselves, since there never seems to have been an official executioner. The ones on the stairs, for instance. Going upstairs in this house is a leisurely and lengthy journey, broken by unexpected turns and landings, and somebody must have decided long ago that it would be nice to break it in another way, by hanging an occasional picture on a level with the passing eye, but never interesting enough to distract it dangerously from the passing foot. A very good rule for stairway pictures, I maintain, who still go up and down a hundred times a day without even a glance at those landscapes where nothing ever happened to me or at those friends in a youth I cannot remember. Yet it gives me a pang to think of seeing Melrose Abbey anywhere but opposite the top step, or Mrs. Donelson, in her blue silk and seed-pearls, no longer on the landing.

I don't believe I ever knew just how we happened to have Mrs. Donelson's portrait, except that my mother, who was very fond of her, must at one time have admired it; and certainly I never knew her when she resembled it, if she ever did. The artist endowed her with an expression of smugness at variance with her youth at the time he painted her and completely at variance with her character at any age. She was older than my mother, and the countless little wrinkles I remember about her mouth and eyes could only have come from wearing all her life too much " expression."

She was charming in what I always think of as the eighteenth-century manner, with a surface brightness that gave all it had all the time. Nobody ever saw Mrs. Donelson reading a book or laying up reserves of any kind against a day or even an hour of drought or dullness. She never needed to replenish the source from which her spirits and her conversation flowed, and sparkled really, in an inexpensive way. I cannot remember a time when I did not find this enchanting, nor do I remember at just what age I began to recognize a certain buoyancy in Mrs. Donelson's facts that made it difficult to pin them down or fit them in with the plodding experience of other people.

She lived in Oxford, Mississippi, and I knew almost as soon as I knew anything about her that her house was supposed at one time to be haunted; that her guests used frequently to appear at breakfast wan and heavy-eyed from their night's experience — just because, she said, she had forgotten to tell them that her houseboy Sam (well over seventy) was a confirmed somnambulist and liable to come into their rooms with his basket of silver and begin setting the table on them while they slept — or rather while he slept and they lay awake in frozen horror, feeling articles of varying shape and heaviness put down on the bed and taken up again by a shadowy figure moving round it.

" It's the clinking noise that frightens them so; they think it must be chains," Mrs. Donelson used to say when she told the story, years before my time. She had long since ceased to mention it and the houseboy Sam had passed to a sleep that knew no walking before my earliest appreciation of her conversation began. There were newer things for my growing interest to feed upon, and I looked forward with avidity to her visits, which usually took place shortly after her trips to New York, while the hats and dresses she went there twice a year to buy still held their original interest in her eyes — those eyes that never ceased to dance at the piping of spring colors or soften at the touch of winter plumes and furs.

Clothes were so immensely important to her that it

made her own seem memorable. I recall as lovingly as if it were an apple tree the green taffeta cape that rustled through one April visit, and the Paris hat with the russet rose and " fall " of black lace is a recollection more accentuated still, though that may be for other reasons; for that was the hat she had had copied " almost verbatim " for Linda Price, at some sacrifice to herself in the beginning and at what might have been the sacrifice of Linda in the end, if the social system in which the two ladies moved had been geared less faultlessly.

It was in the afternoon of her last day in New York, she told us, and she was right in the midst of packing, with all her fall shopping behind her — except that most of it was right there in the hotel room tumbling about her ears — when Linda Price's special-delivery letter was brought in to her. She tore it open and ran her eye over it enough to see that it was all about things at home in Oxford, and was on the point of laying it aside for a more leisurely reading later on, when she noticed a postscript hastily written on a separate half-sheet of paper which seemed to demand instant attention.

It demanded far more than that. It meant, Mrs. Donelson said, that she must stop her packing then and there and go back to Fifth Avenue and buy a hat for

Linda Price — all in the name of friendship, which she confessed hardly seemed worth it at the moment.

"Just whatever you think would suit my coloring," Linda had scrawled across the top of the page. And what exactly was Linda's coloring? Mrs. Donelson couldn't seem to remember. She had started a medium blonde of course — everybody did — but what had happened since? Not as gray as she was herself anyhow; Linda must be a good three years younger. . . .

In the end she decided to do something " really beautiful " and have her own Paris model copied for Linda — only with a pink rose, as a glowing tribute to those three years. It would have to be sent after her, of course, but Linda would think it worth waiting for, she felt, on a bright wave of enthusiasm unshadowed by foreboding.

"But shopping for other people is a pitfall and a gin," Mrs. Donelson said solemnly; " and what is that other thing about a man's foes being those of his own household? It was bound to have been somebody in Linda's house or in mine — and I know it wasn't mine — that caused all the trouble."

She had been at home only a day or two and the hat had not yet arrived when she met Linda Price on the street and told her what she had done.

"What hat do you mean?" Linda asked.

"The one you wrote for, of course," Mrs. Donelson answered.

"But I didn't," Linda said.

There is always a lot of spade work to be done before a misunderstanding of this nature can be — by no means cleared up, but got into a light where it can be considered at all, and so, Mrs. Donelson told us, she took Linda into a store where they could sit down and really go into the matter of the mysterious commission. She promised Linda to find the letter, but in the meantime made Linda promise she would under no circumstances keep the hat unless she really wanted it.

But about that Linda felt no doubt whatever, "Let me know the minute it comes and I will send right over for it," she said in parting.

And indeed when the box arrived Mrs. Donelson had barely time to open it and verify the perfection of her purchase before Aggie, her colored maid, came bounding in to say Mis' Price had done sent for her hat.

"I thought it was funny not to hear from her right away," Mrs. Donelson said, "but I didn't hear a word from Linda till I met her two days later at Kate Speare's luncheon, and then — my dear, you aren't going to believe this — when I asked her how she liked her hat, she said: 'Oh, has it come? Why didn't you let me know?' She had never got the message; she hadn't sent for the hat, and to this good minute she hasn't the remotest idea who came for it. And it doesn't do either of us any good to keep asking the servants; it only hurts their feelings and makes them stubborn. I suppose the best thing we can do is just to forget about it; but there is always that question of the money. I don't so much mind paying for two hats if I have to, but I know Linda doesn't want to pay for none."

"But the letter," we reminded her; "didn't you find it? Couldn't you at least show her she had ordered the hat?"

"Well, that is funny too," Mrs. Donelson said. "The only part of that letter I couldn't find was the half-sheet about the hat. It must have fallen under something in all that welter of tissue paper and boxes back in the hotel room."

I felt at the time and I still feel that I would give a good deal to see that half-sheet of paper; or the messenger who called for the hat; or the hat, for that matter. There has always been something rather fourth-dimensional about this story that seemed to me to merit investigation, but I believe it was never investigated at all. It was several years after she told it before I saw Mrs. Donelson again — years in which I had been too far away to hope for any new light upon it; but that was the first thing I did hope for when I found myself once more in her delightful presence.

"Do tell me," I asked her, "the end of your story about the hat. Was the mystery ever cleared up?"

"What story, dear?" she said.

"About your friend Linda Price's hat," I began again; "the one you bought for her in New York and never knew who got it."

Mrs. Donelson looked at me brightly and shook her head. "Not my story, dear, but I like it; do go on," she urged.

# SUMMER'S END

THIS MORNING as soon as I got up I went out and looked at the fig bushes and stood there wondering how much earlier I would have to be in order to beat the birds and the peacocks to the ripe ones. The whole summer can go by sometimes without a single soft and juicy fig falling to my share.

I was consoling myself with some that merely looked ripe and hadn't fooled anything else when I saw Edna Hillman approaching in her high-heeled pumps with a book under her arm. It was *So Red the Rose*, which she has borrowed off and on since the date of its publication and had now walked over in the cool of the morning to exchange for another selection.

We have been Edna's lending library for so long that she has, several times over, exhausted all the lighter veins on our shelves. We have never had enough novels to keep her what she would call "in," but she has no objection to taking on her favorites for a third or even a fourth round rather than venture into other realms than fiction.

I offered her a fig and she said it wasn't ripe, which I knew already, and that she didn't like them green, after which she went on to discourage me further by telling me how Papa used to tie every one of his up in a little bag until it was as sweet as sugar.

"Papa was just like you about the birds. He wouldn't ever let anybody shoot one of them. He didn't even like to shoo them away," Edna said.

Often in the late summer — it is late summer now — I remember Edna's father, even without Edna to remind me, and how he used to come over and bring us offerings from his early and imperfect harvest — a basket of Grimes' Golden, which are never golden in this region, or a quart jar of the honey which our local bees do not know how to make. I suppose it is the heavy bloom of goldenrod and ironweed which so discolors the nectar that they brew and makes it taste so sour in spite of being so sweet. I do not remember his figs, but I dare say they were fine if he managed to keep the birds off of them — and I dare say they were few if he did it by tying them up in bags.

Edna lives about a mile away from us, in the house where she was born, a small house with two rooms and a hall and kitchen, and a front porch that was always cool and shady until Mrs. Hillman got to worrying for fear the oak tree at the corner might blow down and kill them and had it sawed down instead.

This seems to be a natural process in the minds hereabout: to select the shelter of a giant tree to build in — where no dwelling is ever too mean and poor to be without grace (Hunding's *Hütte* was charming, I am sure) — and then to grow afraid of it and cut it down.

Every time I went to the Hillmans' house after this sacrilege and saw the stump, larger than the table where they ate their meals, with the richly colored rings that marked its solid age, I would remember how the oak has always been the symbol of strength and think how feeble this one's chances had been in the hands of Mrs. Hillman, who felt safer rocking in the sun.

I was sure that Mr. Hillman felt bad about his tree — perhaps because he never spoke of it. He was rather silent in regard to most things, when you came to think of it — maybe feeling bad about them too. He was always busy with his beehives and his orchard, but they were certainly not remunerative and there must have been some small income from another source. Mrs. Hillman was obviously not bread-winning as she rocked on the porch, and Edna in those days was doing nothing except growing up.

She did not grow up pretty. Even her brown curls could not help out her sallow little face, and the high-heeled pumps she already affected added a touch of real deformity to her adolescent legs; but when she told me one summer that her ambition was " radio " and that Papa was getting her an " upright " so she could " take music," I had occasion for the first time to notice her hands and saw that they were very nice indeed. From her father's side of course, I thought; Mrs. Hillman could never have had these or anything to hand down.

The piano lessons had not gone very far when they had to stop because Mr. Hillman got sick and the money had to go to doctors. Edna was learning a Brahms waltz at the time, and I have never heard it since without thinking of her father sitting on the porch (he had the rocker with the red checked cushions now) that last September before he died, looking over at his orchard, where the speckled apples were already falling and his beehives were almost hidden in the weeds.

Time was going very fast for me just then (I have never believed it ever really goes slowly for anybody) and we were spending all we could of it abroad. I could not have said, without stopping to count, just how long it had been since I saw Edna or her mother, when one afternoon Mrs. Hillman came over for a visit, the object of which she immediately announced.

" I heard you were bringing back a lot of things with you this time," she said, seating herself voluminously (she had grown too " comfortable " for even a pretense of corsets) and looking about her with unfeigned interest, " and I wondered if you were thinking of selling off some of the ones you had already. I thought maybe there might be an art-square you could let me have." (Everybody might not have known that an art-square was a decorated rug for the middle of the floor; I did, though I did not have one.)

I told her I was sorry, and she went on to give me her ideas about interior arrangement and tell me how much " improvements " had always meant to her. " But I like old things too," she added. " I have always been sorry about the clock — Sir John Gilbert's clock. Edna ought to have had that, but they gave it to the Princess Mary for a wedding present. The only thing Edna has is the minatchure."

I was glad she was scrutinizing my new lamp-shade

[ 213 ]

and not my face as she said this, for my astonishment was past concealing. I could not believe I had actually heard the words until by a judicious manipulation of the conversation I had led her to repeat them. She would be glad to show me the miniature any time, she said. A man had offered Mr. Hillman a hundred dollars for it once, but he wouldn't sell it. " Foolish, I call it, but Edna says she wouldn't sell it even now if she got the chance, no matter how much they offered her."

" Who is it a picture of? " I asked her. " Someone in Mr. Hillman's family? "

" I reckon it is. It's real old. There's something in Sir John Gilbert's will about it. Maybe you'd like to see that too some day when you have time. It's pretty long."

I was sure there must be a catch somewhere in this story and I was so curious about it that I planned to avail myself of Mrs. Hillman's invitation right away. I thought a sight of the heirlooms, provided they really existed, was the only thing that would enlighten me. But as it happened, some months elapsed before I had the opportunity of seeing them, and then it was Edna who brought them over to show to me.

Time had made no improvement in Edna. She was still sallow and rather knobby, and the wind-blown bob that had supplanted the curls was a further detraction, but she had never seemed to consider herself at a disadvantage. She was not gay exactly; I should rather say glib, and facetious at all costs.

"Mamma said you wanted to see this old junk, so I brought it over." So saying she handed me the little pasteboard box that contained the family treasures.

I should have had to know a great deal more than I ever have on such subjects to say whether the miniature was one of the really good ones, but certainly it looked so to me, and the will, which was, as Mrs. Hillman had warned me, a somewhat lengthy document and written in a fine old hand, was so brown and brittle and difficult to read that no one could have doubted its authenticity for a moment.

In it the undersigned John Gilbert (whose baronetcy seemed to have been conferred upon him by Mrs. Hillman) bequeathed his very considerable substance to a rather numerous family, but Edna had no idea from which of the sons or daughters her own branch descended, and neither her possession of the miniature nor her failure to possess the clock gave me any clue. Poor Princess Mary may have been showered with most of the antique clocks in the kingdom, but there was no mention of this one in the will. The miniature had been left with various other articles of personal adornment "to my wife Eliza." It was easy to assume that the young man whose charming portrait lay in my hand was one of the said Eliza's sons, but there was no reference to that effect.

"Is it ivory or enamel?" I said, reaching for the reading-glass on the table.

"Bone, most likely," Edna suggested disparagingly. "Bonehead. Look at that hair. And his shirt; I reckon he must have had a sore throat to make him go around with his neck wrapped up that way."

I realized that these and other gibes at the dress of an earlier period were Edna's means of escape from the burden of her pride. I tried to strike a truer note by mentioning that it might be an advantage to have an expert evaluation of the portrait.

"Who knows?" I said. "It may be worth a great deal more than a hundred dollars. Even if you never want to sell it, you might borrow money on it if you should ever need it. You might even let this young man pay for your musical education."

I made the suggestion lightly and was surprised at the suddenness with which Edna leaned over and took the miniature out of my hand. "There wouldn't anybody want to pay for the noise I make," she said, and I did not pursue the subject any further, except to ask her a little about her music.

She said she was "going on with it," but when she played for me, as she presently did, I could see that it was not far. She got through several pieces — the Brahms waltz among them — but the nice hands on the piano were handsomer than they did.

It was after this — I have forgotten how long after — that she began to borrow books and become what she called an " omniverous reader." I used to try sometimes to bring the ladies and gentlemen of her literary revels into our conversations, but whatever impression they made on her was not to be shared, apparently, and as far as I could make out, a diet composed exclusively of romance left all her commonplaces quite unleavened.

I believe now I was mistaken about this. Something must have been preparing her for the romance that has this summer bloomed and faded, while I on the other hand was so little prepared for the form it took that I hardly knew what was happening right under my eyes. They look back differently now on the responsibility of furnishing all those guides and manuals. She was bringing back *Beau Geste* for the third time when she met Stephen. I may even say I was the one (under Providence, of course) who furnished Stephen.

He had been here only a little while when she saw him first, but already long enough to settle into several agreeable habits, one of which was to spend a half-hour or so at the piano after lunch, running over the little songs he had learned in his French boyhood. He did not

[ 217 ]

take his music seriously, but I liked it better than his painting, and as soon as it began I would get my book and go to the hammock where, awake or asleep, I could still listen. I must have dozed off pretty soundly on this particular afternoon, for I did not hear Edna's heels on the gravel as she passed me on her way to the door, and she evidently did not see me lying there or she would have been sure to come over and wake me up. Everybody always does. Such a public performance as sleeping in a hammock is not entitled to consideration and never gets any. " Are you asleep? " is the long-distance formula of approach, shouted, just in case you should be; and the answer is naturally in the negative. This time, however, I was not accosted, and I realized afterward that it was because Edna's eyes as well as her ears must have been strained in the direction of the music.

She had come over as usual to change books, walking in her pumps through the midsummer dust, and when a little later I woke up and went into the house, she had already chosen her novel, but she had not gone. She was standing by the piano, where the music had stopped but Stephen still sat, with his hands on the keys, laughing at something she must have said.

It was a little scene that was due for rather frequent repetition during the weeks that followed, with trifling variations. Sometimes the music would not stop, and sometimes Stephen would be painting instead, as she passed and paused and made what overtures her code of etiquette permitted.

It was plain to me from the first that she had never seen anything like him; it must have been plain to him. I used to wonder how his own code permitted him to go on dazzling her so completely and do nothing about it — run away and hide when he saw her coming if he could think of nothing better. Was he studying more of the local psychology?

He said something on that first evening that showed me he was at any rate trying to grade Edna in our social scale. He could not place her with what he called the "planter class" he had been visiting, and certainly not with the sharecroppers he was painting; she must belong somewhere in the vast space between, hitherto unpeopled by his imagination.

"She reads a good deal for a girl like that, doesn't she?" he asked me.

"Like what?" I asked back.

"Oh well, where would she belong exactly?"

It had been a long time since I had thought of the clock and the miniature and "Sir" John Gilbert, but I thought of them now and told Stephen about them. I felt that the story might teach him, as well as anything could, the futility of applying his system of classification to our loose social structure; but all his interest centered immediately on the miniature. He asked me a dozen questions, which I was totally unable to answer, about the style and character of the workmanship, and the next time Edna came over he walked home with her to see it for himself.

I was afraid he would come back disappointed, but instead he was exceedingly enthusiastic. "It looks like an Englehart—or it might be a Cosway," he said; "only I believe they both signed theirs. Anyway, I have got to examine it under a glass. Whosever it is, it has no business to be where it is now. If I had any money I would buy it."

I told him I didn't believe Edna would sell it no matter how much he had, and reminded him of the way her father had felt about it. I was sure Edna had inherited the ideas along with the picture.

"Well, I suppose that is rather sporting of her, but hard on the picture just the same. It ought to belong to someone who could appreciate it."

"Isn't love a form of appreciation — or sacrifice?"

"In art? Certainly not. Nobody should be sentimental about a work of art."

We had other conversations on the subject, and Stephen paid the picture other visits, while Edna continued to visit him. I don't believe she read the books any more before she brought them back. But it was all very harmless and beginning to be a little dull, and I was thinking how all the summers here — even if they are weaving a romance, even if they are weaving a war — are just like all the others, long and still, when suddenly the headlines broke upon us and nothing was the same.

Stephen began at once the work of crating up his pictures. He had an immense amount of packing to do, for he had been collecting things all summer, and was too busy for much in the way of final conversation, but on the morning before he left I went into his room to take him the cotton bolls Joe had picked for him and a few " American walnuts " shaken down from the tree in the pasture. They were still in their green husks and I was afraid they would stain his clothes if he put them in his trunk, but he wanted to take them and stuffed them into the toes of some of his shoes; then slipping his hand under a pile of ties and handkerchiefs in the tray, he pulled out a small object and held it up for me to see.

" Have a last look," he said. It was the miniature.

With something rather like the instinct of self-preservation I asked him if he was taking it to trace its history for Edna, to find out if it was a genuine masterpiece; but I knew all the time at what a straw I was clutching. I hadn't even the hope that he would lie about it.

"Oh, of course I will find out all I can about it, sooner or later," he said easily, "but I know already it is a masterpiece and it's worth just as much to me no matter who painted it. It's mine now. Edna gave it to me yesterday."

"But she can't afford to — I mean you mustn't let her!" I was really upset.

"What do you mean by 'can't afford to'?" he asked curiously. "She had no idea of selling it; you told me so yourself; and she certainly couldn't sell it to me, because I have no money. Besides, she wanted me to have it."

"Did you tell her you could appreciate it better," I said nastily, "or what did you tell her?" But I knew too well he did not have to tell her anything, and I shifted my ground; I pointed out to him that the picture had a recognized value for whoever owned it, whether it was sold or not, and that Edna was that much poorer for the loss of it.

"Aren't you talking rather about price?" he said. "The value of a work of art is something entirely different, as I see it, and depends more on its being studied and understood. To be shut up in the bureau drawer over there at the Hillmans' would lessen the value of anything."

I could see it was hopeless, but I continued to try, before the expressman came for that trunk, to stir up some sort of conflict in Stephen that would result in his leaving the miniature behind. My arguments had for him no substance whatever, and they even began to look a little spectral to me by the time I abandoned them.

Perhaps my values really were misplaced, my emphasis put on the less important things. Should not a maiden's heart be of more worth than a miniature? Yet I thought little and said nothing about poor Edna's heart, which he was taking with him as surely as any specimen in his trunk. . . .

I was wondering about her heart as we stood there by the fig bushes this morning. Wherever she wears it, it is certainly not upon her sleeve and I have no way of knowing what the summer did to it. I am glad she hasn't as large a past as mine for things to fall into and be lost, because then to think of Stephen as " somewhere in France " would put him not only miles but years — another war — away; beyond the reach of my reproaches, should any better ones occur to me, or her forgiveness, should it ever occur to her that she has anything to forgive.

# DEATH
## AND THE MAIDEN

I NOW HAVE a bat in the house. I don't mean a mere transient bat, flying in and flying out again, and everybody chasing him with brooms and blankets the way they do in the country. I don't know how this one got in, but he shows every intention of being a permanent resident, hiding away discreetly during the daytime and only coming out after the lamps are lighted, and then only occasionally, and winging his way from room to room quite close to the ceiling, where he will be as little in the way as possible. And that, since the ceilings are so high, is really very little — or would be except for the odd shadows he throws and for a sort of general feeling that he ought not to be there. Or ought he? That is just the question. I don't know how to place him symbolically as I would a raven, or even a plain bird. So far we have never had a raven, and we have lived down the idea that a bird in the house is the sign of death; birds get in too often here to be a sign of anything except that somebody has left the door open. Some of them have their nests in the vines, where they can step right in, as it were, but most of them are migratory birds, only lodging with us for a night or two on their way somewhere else, and so, not knowing very well where they are anyhow, they are always terribly confused if anybody turns on the porch light or comes up in a car with its headlights reflected in the windows and the glass doors. Then they begin to fly about and dash themselves against the panes in the most suicidal manner. One evening not long ago I opened the front door to a visitor and found him standing with his hat in one hand and a bird in the other, which he presented to me as if it were a calling card; but most of my friends are not so quick as that and let the birds in with them. After that they have to be kept out of the fire and poked down from the picture frames, and much liveliness ensues before the business of a call can be got down to. They have really helped me out on various occasions that might have been dull without them; but I feel different about this bat. I hope he will confine his appearances to the evenings when I am alone.

I wonder just how superstitious I really am. Not so much perhaps as I like to think, but there must be for me some lurking atavism in the nonsense or I wouldn't find it so interesting. Signs and portents are at their best when they are half believed in — but only half, for me again. If I had to give them their fatal value I should shrink from them utterly, I am sure, in my usual cowardly fashion. Everybody may not feel this way perhaps; at least there was a time when everybody didn't. They could look a bad omen in the face just as they would a disagreeable fact and deal with it accordingly.

My cousin Bettina was like that. I have never known anyone who believed in as many dire presages as she did, and was so undismayed by any of them. She used to visit us for months at a time when I was a child, and I have often wished that while I was learning the things about her that seemed thrilling and romantic to me then, I had learned something about courage, which seems to me now the most thrilling romance in the world.

Meeting Cousin Bettina at the station was almost the biggest excitement of my country childhood, owing in large measure to the number and the nature of the pieces of baggage that descended to the platform in her wake. I believe that even today a guest with little baggage has for children, at the outset anyway, little charm.

She was almost the oldest person we knew, but she was a seasoned traveler, and with her came, in addition to her satchel and her lunch basket, her bandbox and umbrella, and sundry bundles varying in size and shape from year to year, one article that overshadowed all the rest in magnitude and interest: a large guitar in a green baize cover, to which she always referred as the Instrument. " Who has the instrument? . . . Oh, there it is. . . . Don't lean against the instrument, children." It was obliged to go by hand because, like My Grandfather's Clock, it was too tall for her trunk, and though it was never " touched " in a musical sense (it still possessed a string or two, as we had ascertained by peeping inside the green baize cover), in the line of travel it was heaved into day coaches where it had to stand erect in corners, and into sleepers where it could sometimes recline, and it always went, for the reason that it was too precious to leave behind.

We knew that this was because it had belonged to Cousin Bettina's lover — the only one she had ever had, or needed, since she had elected to love him permanently.

He was a young man of some genius and much charm, a Polish naturalist who had come to this country somewhat in the footsteps of Audubon; and there were rumors persisting down the generations that he had never in full measure returned Cousin Bettina's devotion, else why had she not prevailed against the wave of national enthusiasm that had swept him back to Poland? Perhaps she did not try; she may have encouraged his patriotic responsiveness. Certainly she could not have continued to adore a living man as she adored the dead hero he presently became in one of those wars or near-wars with which Poland has been always so ready to gratify the ardors of her sons.

So barefaced had Cousin Bettina's attachment become with the years that even we children were permitted to make free with it. We probably felt instinctively that she liked to be reminded of it.

> Unless you can muse in a crowd all day
> On the absent face. . . .

She used to read Mrs. Browning aloud a good deal, skimming the creamy sentiment coolly in her pleasant voice, and I adored to listen.

"Were you ever in love like that, Cousin Bettina?" I asked when the poem had come to an end, thinking I knew just what she would answer and hoping there would be a good deal of it. But one never did quite know.

" I am in love like that now," she said with exquisite brevity.

I believe she remembered everything Ladislas had ever said to her, and it was fortunate that what he said was so often worth recalling. His early life in Poland, about which he had told her a great deal, would not seem less interesting today and I wish I could remember better in my turn the account of it that was handed down to me. Why do we so seldom put these things in writing before it is too late? Why do we not seize and save them before they go down for the third time? As long as there are people to remember them they seem to have somewhere an existence of their own that would always be in some way recoverable; then all at once we realize that by being forgotten they have ceased to be at all.

Ladislas found many things in this country that reminded him of Poland, Cousin Bettina said. In the evening when the frogs would begin their melancholy concert on the pond, it made him homesick. " *Ça me fait de la nostalgie,*" he would say with a far-away look on his face; and once when the wild geese flew over, he told her how, when he was a boy, he used to watch the cranes, hundreds of them together, their long legs like

rudders to guide their flight, and he repeated a translation he had made from a poem by Krasinski:

> Their feet with soil from Poland's fields were shod,
> And I was sad, O God. . . .

The house on his family estate must have been extremely old, and there was not a room in it, he told her,
where something terrible had not happened — terrible
in the Polish, almost the medieval sense of violence and
blood. And not only the tragedies in his family but its
more peaceful closing scenes were always faithfully fore-
told, he assured her, by such omens as the untimely
crowing of cocks or ticking of watches or, most infal-
libly of all, by the howling of wolves.

"I think when my time comes I may hear them too,"
Cousin Bettina said. "Wherever Ladislas is, he knows
that in spirit I am his next of kin."

"Do the wolves know it too?" my father asked her.

It was no doubt this conversation or some other like
it that gave my brother, who at that period of his life
was something of a virtuoso in sound-effects, the idea
of getting out of bed one snowy night and emitting
wolfish howls under Cousin Bettina's window. He was
so immediately hauled in by my father that we hoped
she had not heard him, but the next morning at break-

fast she remarked, apropos of some catastrophic headlines in the paper:

"I have never entertained the same fears that other
people seem to have in regard to death; least of all my
own." She glanced round the table as she spoke, and the
faded beam of her blue eyes rested on my brother. " But
I do hope you were well wrapped up, Robert. I was
uneasy for fear you might take cold."

As I look back from my mature standpoint on various
incidents connected with Cousin Bettina, I feel sure she
was sincere in saying she did not share the common
view of mortality nor feel the customary shrinking from
any of its manifestations. " I do not mind dead people,"
she used to say, and she had of course known many.
She did not grieve for them unduly when they were her
own, nor reject in any way the knowledge that she
would some day be one of them. It may be she had
" mused " so much on Ladislas, to whom death had
come in its most approved form (*dulce et decorum
est . . .*) that all death had lost some of its disfavor in
her eyes; but whatever its cause, it was a state of mind
that made for courage, even in little things.

She had no home of her own, and her life was spent
in journeying back and forth to the homes of others.
This operation she called " flitting," which was surely a

propitiatory term for railway travel in the South of those days; and not only its tediousness but all its odd contacts and predicaments, and even its occasional dangers, she seems to have met with perfect coolness and a sort of light dignity that never forsook her. On one occasion she spent the whole night by herself in a lonely little station, and on another in the company of a lunatic who thoughtfully locked the door on the inside and pocketed the key. I think she was a little proud of the time when the doors of the passenger coach got jammed in a collision and she heard the conductor say to a man who was breaking the window with his boot heel: "You all would do a whole lot better to quit your screamin' and scufflin' and go sit back in your places like that lady over yonder with the *gui*tar."

One of her experiences which we loved to make her tell still seems to me to have been about as neatly combined to freeze the blood as anything I have ever heard, and rather substantiates, I think, her claim of not minding dead people.

It happened near the little town of Lagrange, now not quite so small nor so far away as it was that winter evening when she found herself obliged to stay-over there because the train to Memphis was snow-bound somewhere else, and to stay in the waiting-room at the station because the one small hostelry the town afforded

had so repelled her at the first breath she drew within
its stained and clammy walls. At least there was a stove
in the waiting-room, red-hot about the middle, and a
big box of sawdust to contain the brown juices that had
flowed so unconfined inside the " hotel," and the telegraph operator would no doubt be there all night, paying an intermittent attention to the clicking of the
wires. It might easily have been worse, she thought,
looking back over a rather vast experience as she settled
herself in one corner of her bench and prepared to doze
away what she could of the long hours ahead of her.

It was still early in the evening, though already dark
outside, when a gentleman came in, stamping the snow
from his polished boots. He was not young; middle-
aged, she thought, from what she could see between his
hat-brim and the folds of his black silk muffler; and it
was evident that he had not come to meet a train, but
to send several telegrams which he held already written
in his hand.

She could not hear the low-voiced exchange of remarks between him and the operator, but she was sure
that some of them had reference to her presence there,
and as he turned to go he stepped over to where she sat
and inquired with much politeness if there was anything he could do to mitigate the discomfort of her
situation.

"Naturally you could not relish the hotel," he said, "but this seems very bad. The Memphis train may not come before the middle of the forenoon."

She thanked him with her customary composure, dispelling as always with her first words any wandering-minstrel impression her odd belongings might have created. The Instrument stood erect beside her, but was not a barrier to the gentleman's hospitable intentions.

"My home is about thirty minutes' drive out of town," he said, "but there are rugs in the buggy; you would not take cold, and my sister who keeps my house for me would make you welcome —" He paused, and then, before Cousin Bettina could thank him, continued: "But I should tell you first, though I hope it will not influence your decision, that my home is at present a house of mourning. My son died this morning. I am here to send some messages regarding his funeral. This weather makes it difficult for the friends who would like to come."

Cousin Bettina expressed her sympathy, and the telegraph clerk, who had been listening in friendly silence, now spoke a friendly word. "Better go, ma'm," he said; "Colonel Wilkinson can put you up fine." And indeed Cousin Bettina, sincerely thankful for the offered kindness, was already gathering up her possessions and straightening her bonnet.

Colonel Wilkinson's house was set back at some distance from the road, and it was only after they had turned in at the open gate that she could see its lighted windows between the trees. There were many lights, upstairs and down, and the coal fires burning in the open grates gave to the whole interior, as they entered, that appearance of warmth that is often better for the spirits than warmth itself. It did not look like a place of sorrow, and Cousin Bettina, who was soon sitting with a cup of tea, steaming her wet little shoes by the hearth in the library, felt the contrast with the station bench almost too keenly.

The door into the front parlor stood open and she could see candlelight on white chrysanthemums. Family and friends passed in and out; neighbors came and went; and all were invited to approach the bier where the son of the house was lying, in the white robe the custom of those days approved. Cousin Bettina was invited too and stood for a moment looking down at the quiet face of the young man, who, being young and being dead, seemed to her to resemble Ladislas.

It had stopped snowing and the moon had come out when, a little later, she looked out of the window in the pleasant room assigned to her, down on the lawn with its drifted spaces and burdened evergreens. "Deep," she thought, wondering about the train to Memphis.

But there was no use worrying before morning, so she turned out her lamp and got into bed.

She dropped off, she said, the moment she closed her eyes, and it seemed to her she had only been asleep a few minutes when she opened them again, but she knew that some time had passed because there was no longer any firelight on the ceiling. She looked at the grate and saw only ashes; yet there was a light from somewhere. The moon? . . . She looked toward the window, and there, standing between the white curtains, she saw the young man she had seen in the parlor downstairs, still in his white robe and holding a lighted candle in his hand.

"He seemed to be looking out of the window," Cousin Bettina said, "but his eyes were closed."

If anybody to whom she told this story ever failed at this point to say: "What did you do?" it was probably from being too breathless to say anything, but Cousin Bettina, it seems, did nothing at all. There was very little time to think about being frightened, she explained, for he turned almost immediately and went out of the room; she could see the candle going down the hall. "Then I felt a little cold, so I got up and shut the door; and then I went back to sleep," she said, "though not immediately."

When she woke again, the sun was shining through

that window and the fire was being rekindled by a
Negro maid kneeling on the hearthrug, who turned as
Cousin Bettina stirred, and smiled cheerfully.

" Looks like Mr. Lewis is goin' to have a fine day for
his funeral after all," she remarked; " an' it sho is a pity
the doctor won't let Mr. Edward go to it — an' them
two boys has done done everything together sence the
day they was bo'ned twins. They was out duck-shootin'
together when they bofe cotch cold, but Mr. Edward
is gettin' over his'n."

So that was it. Twin brothers; and naturally Mr. Edward in his nightshirt had looked like Mr. Lewis in
his shroud. Cousin Bettina wondered if they had ever
gone sleep-walking together; but naturally, she said,
she didn't breathe a word about what had happened.
" I wouldn't have done it for the world; they had all
been so kind. . . ."

I have always wished I knew a little more about just
how that " time " of hers for which she had been so long
prepared finally arrived. She had expected the last
enemy for so many years that he may have surprised
her in the end, but whether from ambush or in the open
field, I am sure she met him with becoming spirit and
I trust that nothing was lacking that could in any way
encourage or console. I even hope there were wolves.

# ELEMENTARY

Hardly anybody seems to last out very long in the contemplation of nature, even at its best; I have noticed that many times. I love the Helen Hokinson picture of the assiduous butler drawing the curtain across the evening sky and saying: "Madame, have you finished with the moon?" One finishes very quickly; the attention wanders and is lost, or settles down comfortably on some detail where it can feel at home.

I remember standing one evening with an artist and a poet by the most beautiful meeting place of shore and

sea that any of us had ever seen — or at least we thought
so at the time and kept saying so, until we finally decided just to be still and listen to the waves, while the
moon rose over Diamond Head and turned the sand
to silver at our feet.

The poet was John Burroughs. I have forgotten the
artist's name, but all at once he exclaimed: "God, I
thought they had it that time!" and John Burroughs
said he thought so too, and I knew what both of them
were talking about because I had been watching it myself. It was a child's tin bucket that had been left on the
sand and was being alternately swallowed and dis-
gorged by the inflowing tide.

That is the kind of thing that is always happening
when I am around, or else I just notice it more.

> The moving waters at their priest-like task
> Of cold ablution round earth's human shores

are always washing away the little buckets, and we
are on the side of the bucket every time. And for all our
practical ends, and certainly for our social occasions,
that is exactly where we should be. Real rapport with
the elements is another matter altogether, and in my
opinion not one to be generally recommended.

I always know when I have been alone with nature
long enough by having her begin to make supernatural

faces at me, and by a tendency to forget that her un-
earthly voices are only wind or leaves, or far-away
freight trains (which might as well be nature) blowing
for grade crossings in the night.

Everybody loves to tell his favorite sound, and I take
pleasure in stating here that this last one is mine. Fortunately almost everybody has heard it at one time or
another and so I do not have to describe how effective
it is, coming from distances of field and forest to wake
us out of sleep. One instantly becomes a divided per-
sonality, half of the mind registering Illinois Central,
say, and the other half whispering things like: " Fade,
fade away and quite forget. . . . Cease upon the midnight with no pain. . . ."

What with viaducts and things, the prolonged ban-
shee utterances I have in mind are hardly to be heard in
cities any more. Some day I suppose they will not be
heard anywhere any more, but I hope by that time to
have made my own grade crossing and ceased upon the
midnight with the voice of my locomotive.

I dare say that if I hadn't lived so much of my life
in the country I might get this same sort of emotional
pleasure out of wind and rain and other elemental dis-
turbances; but as it is, I can seldom forget their real
nature long enough to come entirely under their spell,
knowing too well what morning brings when stormy

nights are over, having too many visions of pink petals being made into pea soup and birds' nests lying on the grass with their little blue eggs scrambled. I often envy the urban state of mind that can just turn over and go to sleep again without feeling that it ought to be up holding an umbrella over something.

The only bad weather I can really enjoy is in books, where I am very partial to it — the worse the better. I never want Sherlock Holmes or Mr. Pickwick to have any but foggy streets and frozen coaches to get about in, or anything but storms for Stevenson's ships. The elements can hardly overdo it for me in literature, but I always prefer them as a background, and not as a stage trick, invoked to intensify a situation. Real weather is not co-operative on that plan, and for myself I am glad of it; my own situation seldom needs intensifying, and I would really rather have things happen at variance with the barometer, as they usually do, it seems to me. I feel reasonably sure that if anything sinister (nice word) should ever befall me, it would not be on one of those whispering nights with ivy tapping on the windows and something else, so far unidentified, groping at the doors, when I naturally expect it. I always remind myself, and it makes me feel much better, that it is sure to be on some beautiful bright afternoon or morning when I do not expect it at all. And two

things that did happen, not long ago nor far away —
just outside the front gate, to be exact — would have
had for me, I imagine, quite an authentic chill if they
had not happened in precisely the kind of weather that
makes it difficult to be afraid of anything.

The first was on an autumn afternoon so flaming
with color that the wood where I was walking with
Jubby seemed as if it might sink to ashes behind us as
we passed along. Except that Jubby wasn't really passing; he kept making side trips off into the vines and the
bushes with his nose to the ground. I called him once
or twice and then forgot him, I suppose, and went on
my way without him. It was not until I had turned and
was coming back by the same path that I saw him again,
and never shall I forget how he looked. He was holding
a large dark object, which turned out to be a brief-case,
in his mouth — holding it by the handle, with his head
thrown back to keep it from dragging, and prancing
like the unicorn through the red and yellow leaves, coming to meet me and lay it at my feet.

It had been hidden in a thicket by some thugs, or at
least thieves, who had camped there in a stolen car; and
it contained all the evidence necessary to land them both
in jail. And I know exactly the kind of day we should
have had to find it in, and am still thankful we didn't,
for I also know how I should have felt scuttling home

# THE YEAR ROUND

LAST NIGHT the moon was new again — harvest moon — hunter's moon? — the dry moon of the waning year, holding her circle like a silver urn from which no drop must spill. There was not even any dew on the lawn, where I used to trail my white dresses when I was a girl and wore them long and kept the laundresses forever ironing ruffles. Walking there last night, with skirts almost to my knees, I thought how nice no dew would be for the ruffles.

I have seen few things in my life that were lovelier to

me than this big house at night with its windows lighted and shining out on that broad sweep of lawn — broader than in daytime because the trees about it seem to have receded into the darkness of the surrounding woods, leaving their empty shadows on the grass. I should like to write about it — to paint it, as one might try to paint a dream. This is light and warmth and human comfort holding its familiar candle steadily against the streaming midnight and the alien stars. . . .

It has become such a symbol to me through all these years that I have reached the point of hating to turn the lights out and giving it over to the dark; and when I turn out the last one, which is the one that throws the bright rectangle of my bedroom window down into a hollow inhabited by beech trees and hoot-owls, I have reached the point of feeling that I have no right to extinguish so lone a beacon — such a star of the deep, as it were. I may even reach the point of letting it burn all night, but at present I am still sensible enough to remember that the beech trees can get on rather well and the hoot-owls rather better without it.

All the same, I am not deceived; I know what flame I would be tending, and against what darkness. I see it sometimes in my dreams.

Only the other night I dreamed again that I came back after one of my long absences, expecting, with every right a dream can give, my usual welcome home. There was no one on the terrace or the steps to meet me, but the doors were open and in I came — on emptiness. . . . I would find them in the dining-room, I said, or in the kitchen; somebody is always in the kitchen. . . . It was strange as only things in dreams are strange, to find the kitchen empty too — the black and white stone floor staring up at me, and the big wood-range that is always burning standing there as cold as some tribal altar whose faith has been put out. And there by the mute, inglorious kitchen stove the horror seized me. I knew now what I should find in all the rooms, but I pursued it to the end and woke to the stricken certainty that there was nobody here at all — not even me.

One should not look for logic in a dream, nor perhaps in the fear from which it rises. Certainly I do not know from what fourth-dimensional perch I could ever see this place so abandoned by the living; yet I have seen it so, and it is strange how all my little casual regrets at the thought of some day leaving a life as pleasant as mine has been — leaving things unfinished, the trowel by the tulip bed, the needle sticking in the seam — are swallowed up in this nostalgic vision. Perhaps everyone has in his mind his own ideal of the perfect sadness; perhaps everyone should have — something so complete that all his minor griefs can be merged in it and need

[ 247 ]

not afflict him individually any more; he has now one thing for which to wear his amulets and keep his tapers burning. . . .

The beech trees down in the hollow where the light from my window falls are at present changing their summer silk (surely the tenderest of all the early greens) for the somewhat rusty garments imposed by the dry autumn. Nature cannot even dry up becomingly, it seems, without plenty of moisture. Even after her flowers and fruit have been laid by, she needs the rains for her own withered cheeks, and this year she isn't having any. All the seasons are full of hazards, and nature is exposed to most of them. Her position is far from strategic.

On the south side of the house where the sundial is, the Virginia creeper has already lost its leaves. In that meridional exposure they were burnt up and thrown away without ever turning red, and that has been another disappointment, for I love to see them running like little threads of flame through the green ivy and encroaching one last time on the dial's face, where they have had to be trimmed back all summer, confusing with their dancing shadows its strict line of shade.

We all go by the "sun clock," as Joe calls it, when we are doing things out of doors. It can be consulted from quite far off, for it stands high against the wall and looks down on us instead of lying on its back where we would have to look down on it; and so it may be said to have a more active part in what goes on around it than sundials usually do. Its motto also, being in English and plainly written, might come in for more attention than the usual cryptogram, except that mottoes if read at all are always read too soon by those for whom they were most intended and lose through familiarity more than they might through strangeness:

WHAT THOU SEEKEST IS A SHADOW

No family, I am convinced, could have profited more than mine by this counsel of detachment — nor have flouted it more consistently. When I look back upon the life that has gone on beneath and about that inscription, it seems laughable in its irony.

Not that we have always borne our disappointments badly or made with too little grace our gestures of renunciation; but that is different from " losing interest," which one might do with shadows, and which no one in this house has ever done. I mean real interest — the kind we give not to new things, but to old ones, the oft-repeated and perfectly understood events that happen here.

That moving finger writing off the hours has never

written off for any of us a day so dull or so despairing that some item of news coming in from the front — a hawk catching one of the baby chickens, for instance, or the cow eating up the English peas — has failed in the impact of its actuality on the generations here residing. Shadow indeed! Are murder, treason, and invasion shadows? What we wanted was guns for the hawk, ropes for the cow, and tears for the chicken; not mottoes. My mother in her youth was often said to resemble the actress Mary Anderson, and I have sometimes wished that the tragic Mary might have seen her crying havoc on one of these occasions.

How would it be, I wonder, if after living a life pitched to this sort of intensity — this sort of absurdity — one could come back and live another as a spectator merely, without trying to do anything about it, no longer expecting things to turn out right, not asking them to promise even, or even to endure, and (less than anything) never calling to them, like the ghost in *Hamlet:* " Adieu, remember me . . ."? It would be an interesting experiment, but I think it could not happen here.

I remember once asking my husband, with whom I was imperfectly acquainted at the time, just why he had wanted to marry me, and being greatly disappointed at his answer, which I felt was less than I deserved. He said it was because I was always happy. Having had most of my life to think this statement over, I am now aware that it was more than anyone has ever yet deserved, and I am sure that what he meant was " interested " — which is not so bad either, and which no doubt I was, having always lived with people who were never anything else.

It is only one of many ways of living, and one little sanctioned by the saints and sages who approve of peace, which it can seldom offer for more than a few minutes at a time; but looking back on peace could hardly be as beguiling to our later years as looking back on some other things: remembering how we laughed though we cannot remember why, and how we wept — for anything — for Hecuba. . . .


Back in the days of the white ruffles, the beaux (we called them that) for whom I wore them had to come so far to see me that they always stayed a long time. They were a great responsibility; they had to be talked to by all the family, and walked about and fed and given books to read, in case they had forgotten to bring one. The ones they brought were always poetry, as I remember; sometimes even Shakespeare; sometimes even Bulwer — according to the beau.

I am afraid it was *The Lady of Lyons* that a young man from Baltimore was reading to me in the shady

parlor one hot summer afternoon when our nice old
John, who was working in the sun, " fell out " and lay
prostrate in the garden walk. My mother was able to
revive him, and the cook to " rest his head " on her
aproned lap, but it needed another man to move him
into the shade, and the only other man on the place just
then was Claude Melnotte, reading away on the parlor
sofa:

... if thou wouldst have me paint
The home to which, could Love fulfil its prayers,
This hand should lead thee, listen! ...

I could hear what was going on in the garden whether
I listened or not, as so could he, but I was too polite to
tell him what we would think of him if he failed to rise
and lend a hand, and this course quite evidently never
once occurred to him — even in retrospect, after both
dramas had ended happily and Bulwer was back in his
pocket and (no thanks to him) John back in the kitchen
drinking buttermilk.

"And do you mean to tell me," a friend of my
mother's said to her, " that you let Anne send that perfectly nice young man all the way back to Baltimore just
because he didn't leap into the garden and pull a dead
nigger out of the sun? " ...

I asked the young daughter of a Princeton professor
not long ago if she knew many boys who really cared

for poetry, and she said she had never known one who didn't; which pleased me very much for I was sure that she had also never known one who would not have leapt into the garden and pulled John into the shade. To my mind this seems to prove something, though I hardly know what; perhaps that I had a more modern outlook on Claude Melnotte than might have been expected of me in those days. I should like to think too that, although so young, I had a good straight eye for values, and that it was living here, where good straight facts have always been so exceptionally intrusive, that gave it to me. . . .

I have been lying in the hammock under the pecan tree, with the squirrels cracking nuts overhead and throwing the shells around. Their granary will never be full at this rate; I don't believe they have one, being thriftless Southern squirrels. Certainly they are not leaving many nuts for me; the stone table is covered with broken shells and kernels and I had to shake what looked like half a peck of them out of the hammock before I could lie down in it.

Again the summer's done — overdone by the almanac — but the days are very warm. There has been no rain for ages, and I lay there with a summer dress on and summer sandals, thinking how thin and dry and brittle the world looked, as if I could crush it in my hand and blow the seeds away. These days with no breath in them seem taken out of time — an interval of strange suspension before the deep respirations begin again.

The peacocks are drooping under the dusty trees, pensively plucking out the last of their last summer's feathers, and the geese move in whispers about their diminished pond. We are all waiting.

This morning I found a limb of one of the ancient crab-apple trees in the garden split and trailing on the ground, and Joe and I have wasted a lot of time trying to prop it up so it would maybe bloom again through one more spring, but we had to give it up at last and get the saw and go in for the work of amputation. It was really a big limb and looked bigger still, lying down on the violets and periwinkle where its shadow used to lie, and I grieved for the pink burden it would never bear again. Perhaps I might try cutting it up and burning it in the fireplace on the first cool evening as a sort of sacrificial offering — to what, I do not know. Apple wood is supposed to be fragrant when it burns, and that sounds pleasantly sacrificial — a sweet savor in the nostrils. I have always found it more agreeable to think of placating a remote Jehovah by giving him something to smell rather than something to swallow.

The garden looks very rusty and forlorn. It too is waiting — for the rain and the late roses that may still come; and Flora, like the apple tree, has a broken limb. She was pushed from her pedestal by some riotous youngsters in the spring and now can only lean against it, waiting too — presumably for some new form of cement, since none that I have ever tried seems worth trying again. . . . One might say by stretching the figure a little that most of the waiting is being done for just that — a new healing for some old abrasion.

In this year, now coming its full circle, whose record I have after a fashion tried to keep, life has been so shot to pieces for so many people that I would hesitate to speak again of any bombs that fell on mine. A year is long enough to learn a great deal about human capacity for readjustment, and no one should need to have a war to teach him — though it does — how ingenious is the human spirit in holding on to the things by which it seems to live. It throws up barricades and shelters of every imaginable sort, one of the most frequent and not the least efficacious being the flimsy pages of some book. What a present help in trouble a good book can be is known to all who read, but maybe only those who write have learned the saving power that lay in many a poor one. To go forth with sorrow and come with beauty

home is a rare experience for an author, but almost anyone can write his way through his troubles and come
out on the other side, even if empty-handed.

I was thinking these things over as I lay in the hammock, when Lucy came across the grass in the preter-
natural silence of her rubber soles, humming a "hymn
tune." I have commanded her to sing as she approaches
so my heart will not miss a beat at hearing a voice out
of nowhere asking if I want my tea hot or cold. Cold,
I told her, with lots of ice — yet here it is, Novem-
ber. . . .

# ANNE
# GOODWIN
# WINSLOW

was born in Tennessee and lived in the country near Memphis until her marriage. Her husband, Eveleth Winslow, of the distinguished naval family of Boston, was an officer in the Corps of Engineers, U.S. Army, and her life with him took her into many lands and places. After his retirement they returned to her old home to live, and, since her husband's death and the marriage of her two children, she continues to spend most of her year there, going to Washington for a few months every winter.

Mrs. Winslow is the author of *The Dwelling Place, A Winter in Geneva and Other Stories, Cloudy Trophies, A Quiet Neighborhood, The Springs,* and most recently *It Was Like This.*

# A NOTE ON THE TYPE

THIS BOOK is set in Granjon, a type named in compliment to ROBERT GRANJON, but neither a copy of a classic face nor an entirely original creation. George W. Jones drew the basic design for this type from classic sources, but deviated from his model to profit by the intervening centuries of experience and progress. This type is based primarily upon the type used by Claude Garamond (1510–61) in his beautiful French books, and more closely resembles Garamond's own than do any of the various modern types that bear his name.

Of Robert Granjon nothing is known before 1545, except that he had begun his career as type-cutter in 1523. The boldest and most original designer of his time, he was one of the first to practise the trade of type-founder apart from that of printer. Between 1549 and 1551 he printed a number of books in Paris, also continuing as type-cutter. By 1557 he was settled in Lyons and had married Antoinette Salamon, whose father, Bernard, was an artist associated with Jean de Tournes. Between 1557 and 1562 Granjon printed about twenty books in types designed by himself, following, after the fashion of the day, the cursive handwriting of the time. These types, usually known as "caractères de civilité," he himself called "lettres françaises," as especially appropriate to his own country. He was granted a monopoly of these types for ten years, but they were soon copied. Granjon appears to have lived in Antwerp for a time, but was at Lyons in 1575 and 1577, and for the next decade at Rome, working for the Vatican and Medici presses, his work consisting largely in cutting exotic types. Towards the end of his life he may have returned to live in Paris, where he died in 1590.

This book was composed, printed, and bound by The Plimpton Press, Norwood, Massachusetts.